Praise for David Novak and *Taking People with You*

"David Novak is a great CEO. A lot of people claim to be good people managers, but David has actually made the investment to train the next generation of leaders at Yum! You will enjoy *Taking People with You* for its commonsense approach to, well, taking people with you."

—Jeffrey Immelt, chairman and CEO, General Electric

"David Novak is an inspiring leader and a very astute student of the art of management."   —Steve Burke, CEO, NBCUniversal

"David Novak has led Yum! Brands to achieve phenomenal business performance. He has accomplished this by being a world-class leader/teacher. His book is a very readable and energizing hat trick combining a compelling personal leadership narrative, great case examples, and pragmatic tools for others to use to build winning organizations."

—Noel Tichy, professor and director, Global Citizenship Initiative at the University of Michigan, and coauthor with Warren Bennis of *Judgment: How Winning Leaders Make Great Calls*

"*Taking People with You* is recommended reading for anyone who wants to learn more about leadership. Whether you want to grow a business or just grow as a person, David Novak's book contains valuable lessons on how to perform at your best and help others do the same."

—Andrew C. Taylor, chairman and CEO, Enterprise Holdings

"David's career is replete with excellent accomplishments in motivating teams and large organizations to achieve the extraordinary. Yum! Brands is a great example. This how-to book distills these lessons so they can easily be adopted by any organization. Just excellent!"

—David Cote, chairman and CEO, Honeywell

"No one exemplifies dedicated personal leadership better than David. He has taught a class in leadership for many years and now is sharing those lessons in his book, *Taking People with You*. David shares his strategies for the kind of meaningful leadership that can move an organization forward and provides examples from his own career and from many other companies including Johnson & Johnson. I highly recommend *Taking People with You* for leaders at all levels in every organization."

—William C. Weldon, chairman of
the board of directors, Johnson & Johnson

"Over the course of my nearly thirty-five-year career, I've worked with many different executives. Few are true leaders. David Novak is one of those rare individuals. Whether you are just starting your career or have already climbed a few rungs, the lessons taught in *Taking People with You* are dead on and should be universally embraced by anyone who wants to get ahead in business or in life. You can't do it alone. And the ride is a whole lot more interesting when you're surrounded by bright people who constantly and respectfully challenge one another to do their best." —Howard Draft, executive chairman, Draftfcb

"Great leaders understand their leadership point of view and are willing to share it with others. That's what David Novak has done for years with Yum! Brands, Inc.—and we are now fortunate enough to have him share his winning philosophies with us. I'm a big David Novak fan and you will be, too, after reading *Taking People with You*—a must read!

—Ken Blanchard, coauthor of *The One Minute Manager*® and *Lead with LUV*

PORTFOLIO / PENGUIN

TAKING PEOPLE WITH YOU

David Novak is the chairman and CEO of Yum! Brands, Inc., which operates in more than 120 countries and employs 1.4 million people. All three of the company's restaurant chains—KFC, Pizza Hut, and Taco Bell—are global leaders in fast food. Prior to leading Yum!, he was president of both KFC and Pizza Hut, and held senior management positions at PepsiCo. Novak has been recognized as "2012 CEO of the Year" by *Chief Executive* magazine, one of the world's "30 Best CEOs" by *Barron's* in 2011 and 2012, one of the "Top People in Business" by *Fortune,* and one of the "100 Best-Performing CEOs in the World" by *Harvard Business Review.* He is also the recipient of the national 2008 Woodrow Wilson Award for Corporate Citizenship.

Thousands of people have already used the teachings in this book to improve their leadership skills and get results. Now it's your turn!

You to You!

D. Novak

✳ *I did my first Yum! cheer on Founder's Day—*
October 7, 1997—the day we were spun off from
PepsiCo, to help launch a new culture filled with fun
and positive energy. Now our people are doing Yum!
cheers around the globe, including these two
thousand restaurant general managers who recently
celebrated their success on the Great Wall of China.

taking people with you

the only way to make BIG things happen

David Novak

PORTFOLIO/PENGUIN

PORTFOLIO / PENGUIN
Published by Penguin Group
Penguin Group (USA) Inc., 375 Hudson Street,
New York, New York 10014, U.S.A.
Penguin Group (Canada), 90 Eglinton Avenue East, Suite 700,
Toronto, Ontario, Canada M4P 2Y3
(a division of Pearson Penguin Canada Inc.)
Penguin Books Ltd., 80 Strand, London WC2R 0RL, England
Penguin Ireland, 25 St. Stephen's Green, Dublin 2, Ireland
(a division of Penguin Books Ltd.)
Penguin Group (Australia), 707 Collins Street, Melbourne, Victoria 3008, Australia (a division of Pearson
Australia Group Pty Ltd)
Penguin Books India Pvt. Ltd, 11 Community Centre, Panchsheel Park,
New Delhi – 110 017, India
Penguin Books (NZ), 67 Apollo Drive, Rosedale, Auckland 0632,
New Zealand (a division of Pearson New Zealand Ltd)
Penguin Books (South Africa), Rosebank Office Park, 181 Jan Smuts Avenue, Parktown
North 2193, South Africa
Penguin China, B7 Jiaming Center, 27 East Third Ring Road North, Chaoyang District,
Beijing 100020, China

Penguin Books Ltd, Registered Offices:
80 Strand, London WC2R 0RL, England

First published in the United States of America by Portfolio / Penguin, a member of
Penguin Group (USA) Inc. 2012
This paperback edition published 2013

1   3   5   7   9   10   8   6   4   2

Copyright © David Novak, 2012
All rights reserved

THE LIBRARY OF CONGRESS HAS CATALOGED THE HARDCOVER EDITION AS FOLLOWS:

Novak, David.
Taking people with you : the only way to make big things happen / David Novak.
p. cm.
Includes bibliographical references and index.
ISBN 978-1-59184-454-9 (hc.)
ISBN 978-1-59184-591-1 (pbk.)
1. Leadership.   2. Employee motivation.   3. Organizational change.
4. Success in business.   I. Title.
HD57. 7. N684 2011
658.4'092—dc23
2011031469

Printed in the United States of America
Set in Adobe Garamond Pro
Designed by Jaime Putorti

To my daughter, Ashley, and all the other people in the world who want to be the best leaders they can be.

A special thanks to all of you who shared your insights and coaching, which helped make this book possible.

All of the author's proceeds will go to the United Nations World Food Programme.

contents

✳ *part one*

GET YOUR MIND-SET RIGHT

✳ *part two*

HAVE A PLAN: STRATEGY, STRUCTURE, CULTURE

* *part three*
- - - - - - - - -
FOLLOW THROUGH TO GET RESULTS

taking
people
with
you

t his book starts with a basic premise: We all need people to help us along the way. You can go only so far by going it alone. If you want to start a business, if you want a big promotion, if you are developing or launching a new product, if you want your company to move in a new direction, if you want to expand your sales territory, if you want to raise money for a good cause, even if you become the coach of your child's soccer team, which has lost every game so far, and you want to show those kids what it feels like to win, you're going to need people to help you get there. You'll never accomplish anything big if you try to do it alone.

Early in my career, I had an experience that changed how I thought about my own role as a leader and inspired me to accomplish what, for me, is my greatest example of taking people with you. I was working for PepsiCo at the time, making my way up through the ranks, and had recently become head of operations for Pepsi Bottling. I had held mainly marketing positions until then, so operations was a new world for me. One of the first things I did was travel to our various plants to meet with the people there and find out more about how things worked.

I was at a plant in St. Louis, conducting a 6:00 A.M. roundtable meeting with a group of route salesmen, when, over coffee and dough-nuts, I asked what I thought was a pretty straightforward question about merchandising, which is all about the displays and visibility we get in convenience and grocery stores. I wanted to know what they thought was working and what wasn't. Right away, someone piped up,

"Bob is the expert in that area. He can tell you how it's done." Someone else added, "Bob taught me more in one day than I'd learned in two years on the job." Every single person in the room agreed: Bob was the best there was. I looked over at Bob, thinking he must be thrilled by all this praise. Instead, I saw that he had tears running down his face. When I asked him what was wrong, Bob, who had been with the company for over forty years and was about to retire in just two weeks, said, "I never knew anyone felt this way about me."

The rest of my visit to the plant went pretty well, but I walked away that day with an uneasy feeling. It was such a shame that Bob had never felt appreciated. It was a missed opportunity for the business, too. We all could have benefited from his expertise, and more people could have learned from him. This guy was clearly great at what he did, but who knows how much better he could have been in a workplace that recognized and rewarded his knowledge. I knew that if he felt overlooked and underappreciated, others at the plant did too.

I've always believed in people, but that experience made me even more determined to be the kind of leader who would never let a person like Bob go through his entire career without being thanked for what he did and encouraged to find out how much more he could do. I wanted the people who worked for me to know that they mattered, and I wanted them to enjoy coming to work every day. I also understood that none of this would happen unless I made it happen. It was my job to cast the right shadow of leadership, because no one else was going to live up to these principles unless I lived up to them first. As a leader, you always have to remember that people tend to follow the leader's actions. You can't say one thing and then do another and expect people to believe in you or follow you. As the leader, you have the opportunity to set an example of how the business should be run.

I am now chairman and CEO of Yum! Brands, the world's largest restaurant company and owner of the brands KFC, Pizza Hut, and Taco Bell. When I started in this position over a decade ago, I thought of the Bobs of the world and made it one of my first priorities to create a recognition culture in which everyone counted and to do it so successfully that our company would become renowned for it. That was no small task, considering we now have more than 1.4 million employees spread out over 117 countries around the world. But while we're far from perfect, it's working. I know it's working, because I get proof of it practically every day.

Today I am probably best known within my organization for casting a shadow of recognition and positive energy. I do this demonstrably by: (1) recognizing people in a unique way for their performance and (2) leading people in our Yum! cheer every chance I get. These two aspects of our culture have traveled all the way around the world. When I first started giving out recognition awards, I decided I wanted them to be much more memorable than your typical plaque or a pen. So when I was at KFC, for example, I gave out these floppy rubber chickens. In my current position, I give out a huge set of smiling teeth mounted on a pair of skinny legs with big feet. Now everywhere we do business, leaders in our organization give out their own versions of these awards. Our HR director in India recognizes outstanding performers by giving them a replica of the Taj Mahal, because the workers who built it are remembered for their passion, determination, and overall excellence. A general manager in Dubai gives out his Camel Award, because camels are revered animals in the desert, known for their steadfastness, perseverance, and undying spirit. The head of our construction department recognizes people with his Shovel Award, naturally, and our chief financial officer has his Show Me the Money Award, which consists of a transparent piggy bank filled with Monopoly money and a copy of the movie *Jerry McGuire,* in which that famous phrase originated. The fact that each leader took the time to personalize these awards makes recognition that much more meaningful and fun for everyone.

I'd also venture to say that most of our 1.4 million people around the world now know and do the Yum! cheer, spelling out the name of our organization: "Give me a Y," the leader will say, and team members will shout back "Y!" and so on. When I first started doing things like these, I was told by some people that my "Western ideas" wouldn't work in places like Asia or Europe. Boy, were those people wrong. I believe that, just like Bob, all people, no matter what they do or where they're from, want to know that they are important and to have fun while they're doing their job. My favorite picture, which now hangs prominently on the walls of our headquarters, features two thousand restaurant general managers proudly doing the Yum! cheer on the Great Wall of China, all of their hands held up high to create the "Y" in Yum! It always reminds me that my shadow has traveled a long way. It also reminds me of the power of taking people with you and the fact that it's the key to achieving breakthrough results. My goal for this book is to share with you everything I've learned about how to lead your team so you can do just that.

Taking People with You is not just another book filled with leadership principles you've heard time and time again. It's really more of an action plan. It offers a very specific process that will help you maximize your potential as a leader and show you how to use your leadership skills to achieve the most important goals you can imagine. It's a book that will force you to look in the mirror and challenge yourself to rise to a higher level. It's a step-by-step guidebook and workbook, and by its end, you'll walk away with a tangible plan that you can use over and over again to get big things done. This is a book that will help you become not just a better leader, but also a better person, by making you more self-aware and showing you how to build up the people around you.

How can I make such bold promises? I'm certain this book can do these things because I have been developing and testing its content for the past fifteen years. This book comes out of a leadership program of the same name that I have taught to more than four thousand people in my organization.

It all started back in 1996, when I was working for PepsiCo as the president of KFC and Pizza Hut. Roger Enrico, who was chairman of the company at the time, called me up and said, "David, I'd like you to create a leadership program for PepsiCo executives. You've got a pretty good reputation for building and aligning teams, and I'd like you to share what you know and what you do with others."

I was really honored and excited by the opportunity, because this is just the sort of thing I love to do. I went to work on the program right away. I had pretty much figured out what I was going to present—I even had a date scheduled to give my very first program to a group of fifteen PepsiCo executives—when I got a phone call that changed everything.

It was Roger again, only this time he had something different to tell me. "David," he said, "we're going to spin off the restaurants." I immediately asked, "What the heck does that mean for our people and our company?"

What it meant was this: PepsiCo was going to keep its packaged foods brands—Pepsi and Frito Lay—but it was going to shed all three of its restaurant brands—KFC, Pizza Hut, and Taco Bell. They were going to spin them off together to become a brand-new, totally independent public company.

I was part of the restaurant side of the business, of course, so it no longer made sense for me to give my leadership program to a group of PepsiCo executives that I wouldn't be working with for much longer. The program got shelved, and I was distracted by other details, like who was going to lead this new company.

It turned out that the answer to that question was me, along with a guy named Andy Pearson, a past president of PepsiCo and a professor at Harvard Business School. I became president and Andy became the chairman and CEO, as well as my mentor even after he retired and I took over his position a couple years later. One of the first things Andy said to me when we were starting out was, "How would you like to have lunch with Jack Welch, the legendary CEO of General Electric, and talk to him about what we're going to do with our new company?"

Of course I said yes. The opportunity to pick the brain of one of the most successful businessmen alive was too good to pass up. I asked Jack every question I could think of and just sat there taking notes as he answered. One of my last questions was, "If you were in my position, about to start a new company, what would you do?"

What he said really hit home. He told me, "Looking back on my career at GE, one of the things I wish I could do over is I wish I would've talked to our people more about what kind of company I envisioned us to be . . . what our values were and what we really stood for."

I went back to my office and spent the next week thinking about how I could do just that.

I wanted us to be a company with a unique culture, one that revolved around a genuine belief in people. I took another look at my leadership program, revised it, and made it part of communicating that message. My goal was to scale the program so that I could reach as many people as possible and make it relevant to a broad audience. There are obviously a lot of people I have to reach when I want to communicate an important message about our company. Launching this program was my first step toward building the unique Yum! culture.

I taught my Taking People with You program for the very first time to a group of just eight executives in London. In the years since then, I have expanded the reach significantly and strengthened the content, constantly adding to it, refining it, and making it better. As CEO of a Fortune 500 company, I've had the opportunity, along with my team, to study best practices and learn from some of the most successful companies in the world. I've interviewed experts like Jim Collins on building great companies, Larry Bossidy on execution, Bob Rotella on the psychology of winning, John Wooden on coaching for performance, Noel Tichy on having a "teachable point of view," and Ken Blanchard on creating a people-first culture. I've sought insights from highly respected active CEOs, like Jamie Dimon, Indra Nooyi, Bill Weldon, Jeff Immelt, Dave Cote, Steve Burke, Randall Stephenson, Andy Taylor, and Alan Mulally. I've also benefited from the wisdom of a prestigious board of directors that includes David Dorman, Ken Langone, Massimo Ferragamo, Jon Linen, David Grissom, Tom Nelson, Bonnie Hill, Tom Ryan, Bob Holland, and Bob Walter. (At the back of this book is a list of people I've sought knowledge from in one way or another, including in-depth, videotaped interviews that I've done with many of them to share with the participants in my leadership program.) In the coming pages, you will see how these people, who are some of the most successful leaders and experts alive today, apply many of the steps in this book to their own businesses.

This book also benefits from the inclusion of interactive tools, which have been provided by two of the most notable thinkers on culture and breakthrough thinking in business:

John O'Keeffe. During a visit to the Yum! division in China a few years ago, I noticed that team members there displayed a tremendous drive for performance. Everyone I talked to had these big goals that they were working on, and they all used language like *step-change* and *breakthrough*. The division was then, and still is, hugely successful, China being our largest and most rapidly expanding market, so I had to find out what this was all about. I asked the head of our China division, Sam Su, and he told me about this Business Beyond the Box training course he had taken in London, given by an international speaker, author, and former colleague of Sam's at Procter & Gamble, John O'Keeffe. Sam had liked it so much that he had the materials translated into Mandarin and personally taught them to everyone on his team. I was so impressed with how the training had worked in China that I wanted everyone in our organization to be exposed to it. Now, thanks to the efforts of our vice president of people development, Tim Galbraith, we have cascaded and taught a version of John's program (which we call Achieving Breakthrough Results) in every corner of our organization. It has become an invaluable part of our training at Yum! Brands. John has generously allowed us to use a number of his tools from that program throughout this book.

Larry Senn. I first met and worked with Larry, founder and chairman of Senn Delaney, when I became the president of KFC in the mid-1990s. Out of the blue, I got a letter from a culture expert who said he had a process, including tools and exercises, that helped people become better leaders and work better as a team. I met with him and was so impressed that I took my KFC team to an offsite meeting in Blackberry, Tennessee, to learn from Larry. They in turn were so impressed that they took the tools to their own team members, and Larry's influence kept spreading until it reached our front-line employees. I used Larry and the Senn Delaney process again when I took over Pizza Hut and in the first years after the spin-off when we used his tools to grow and implement our culture all around the world. Several of my favorites among Larry's tools are included in this book.

* How to Use This Book

I still teach my Taking People with You program regularly—up to eight times a year, in fact, in three-day sessions each time—and people often ask me how, in my position, I can afford to spend so much time on it. I figure that with three famous brands and an international infrastructure already in place, if I can teach our people how to get big things done, then just imagine the potential for even more growth. I'm pleased to say that despite global challenges, Yum! Brands has been growing during these hard economic times. Our stock has increased over six times, and we've had 13 percent growth or more for the past nine years. The fact that our organization has put the lessons in this book into action is a major reason behind our success.

A good leader has to be goal-oriented; otherwise you might end up just leading people around in circles. So I'll start you off in the next chapter with a provocative question: What's the single biggest thing you can imagine that will grow your business or impact your life?

Once you've set a goal for yourself in chapter 1, each subsequent chapter focuses on a single step along the path to achieving it. These steps are divided into three sections: (1) getting into the leadership mind-set, (2) developing a plan and building alignment, and (3) following through, on both the execution of that plan and the support of your people.

At the end of each chapter, you will be challenged to self-reflect on where you stand in relation to the lesson you just read and asked to apply what you learned to your current goal. Each of the book's three parts will end with additional questions to help you turn these lessons into action, so that this becomes more than just a passive reading experience. This is a book you can use to truly grow and improve and reach your goals.

My coaching is that you do *not* sit down and read this book cover to cover in one sitting. If you do, you'll be selling yourself short. This is a workbook on how to get things done better and faster by getting people fired up to help you achieve your goals. To do this right, you need to take your time, reflecting on each step and on your own leadership style. In fact, I suggest that you read no more than one chapter a day. Altogether there are fourteen chapters in this book, which means that in just two weeks, you can be well on your way to being the kind of leader who accomplishes big things. If you're willing to put in the time, I believe this could be one of the most powerful and most action-oriented books you've ever read.

1 * an insight-driven approach to leading people and achieving big goals

you have to begin by asking yourself three big questions that will drive your approach to leadership and allow you to take people with you. They are:

1. What's the single biggest thing you can imagine that will grow your business or change your life?

2. Who do you need to affect, influence, or take with you to be successful?

3. What perceptions, habits, or beliefs of this target audience do you need to build, change, or reinforce to reach your goal?

Before I ask you to answer these questions, I need to explain the right way to approach them. When Roger Enrico first asked me to develop a program on leadership, the request forced me to take a look in the mirror and ask myself what was my key to taking people with me. How, exactly, was I able to get people on the same page and marching toward a goal? I concluded that the core of my leadership success stems from my ability to think like a marketer.

My current title is CEO, but I'm a marketer at heart. I graduated not from Harvard Business School, but from the University of Missouri with a bachelor's degree in journalism and a major in advertising. My first job out of college was as a copywriter at a tiny ad agency in Washington, D.C., that worked on only local business accounts. From those modest beginnings, my career grew to where it is today.

In marketing, if you can get inside the minds of your customers, you have the opportunity to solve their problems for them in a way that can improve your business. You need to have a good understanding of what they're thinking and why they're thinking that way. In order to get people to buy your product, for example, you have to start by gaining insight into what will convince them that they can't or shouldn't live without it. To be a successful leader, one who gets big things done, you need to have the same kind of insight into the minds of those you lead.

To give you an example of how this works in marketing, let me tell you how we turned around Taco Bell several years ago. Taco Bell is our most profitable brand in the United States today, but a number of years ago, we were struggling. As a result, we did a problem-detection study and found out the biggest, most important, and most frequently occurring problem customers had with our brand was that our products weren't portable because they were just too messy. Our tacos, burritos, and nachos just didn't work on the go, and they could easily end up in your lap if you dared to eat and drive. That's a real issue when 70 percent of your business comes from the drive-thru.

Prior to this study, Taco Bell had launched two new products that had been duds in the test market: a quesadilla and a grilled stuffed burrito. We'd introduced them simply by advertising them in descriptive terms, saying Taco Bell now had a new quesadilla and a new larger, grilled burrito. Both products, however, also happened to be very easy to eat on the go because the grilling process sealed the ingredients together in their tortilla wrappers. So we took those same two products and repositioned them as portable and easy to eat. We signed up Jeff Bezos from Amazon as our celebrity spokesperson and advertised the quesadilla as the hottest new "handheld" on the market, a takeoff on the new technology craze that was so appealing to our young target audience. Then we relaunched our Grilled Stuft Burrito as the "heavy-duty portable" with some really funny advertising. And guess what happened? The same two products that had failed before now generated double-digit same-store sales growth. By repositioning them in the context of how our customers were thinking and presenting them as a solution to their major problem with our brand, these products were now a huge success.

We then built on this formula for success by creating our Crunchwrap as the ideal portable product. The ingredients were sealed within an octagonal soft tortilla. Our advertising had customers claim that the Crunchwrap was "Good to Go," and we used a wavelike hand movement that helped the phrase go viral and become part of the vernacular. More important, the Crunchwrap was named "product of the year" by *Nation's Restaurant News* and resulted in tremendous same-store sales growth. Again, by focusing on portability, we created a winner. It was a home-run insight that turned Taco Bell around.

What we did at Taco Bell is what I call reframing. You don't just talk about what you're offering people; you make sure your brand or product is positioned in a way that is relevant to whomever you're trying to influence. This kind of insight-driven thinking works in all kinds of situations. Snickers achieved dramatic growth when it tapped into the consumer mind-set that candy bars are not good for you and started touting their brand as "The Snack that Satisfies." Swatch did something similar when, instead of positioning themselves as simply another watch brand, they realized that consumers wanted to use their watches as clothing accessories. Swatch started offering a wide variety of watchbands, and soon their products became a fashion statement. After the people at Kellogg's Corn Flakes realized that customers had become so enamored with the plethora of new cereal products that they had forgotten about their classic brand, they rejuvenated sales by challenging people to "Taste it for the first time." Pampers revitalized its image and sales by shifting focus from a brand that stood for dryness, which any diaper brand could have claimed, to one that appealed to mothers by emphasizing how much the company cared about the development of their babies. And if you're as old as I am, you may remember how Oldsmobile successfully countered its stodgy image by talking about its new model as "Not your father's Oldsmobile." You get the idea. Knowing how people are thinking gives you the insight you need to reframe your product in a way that gets people on your side.

The great news for you as a leader is that this insight-driven approach doesn't work just with customers; it's the right first step in any leadership situation. For example, Jim Stengel, now a professor at UCLA's Anderson School of Management, told me how he started off his new position as global marketing officer for P&G in 2001 by getting inside the heads of the people he was meant to lead. The company was not in good shape at that time, so he hired a couple of professors to find out why and what effect that was having on the people who worked there.

"We spent time talking to P&G people all around the world," Stengel explained to me. "We wanted to understand what was on their minds, what their pain points were, what winning would look like to them. We used the same techniques we use for brand research on the people within our organization. And what I found was, they weren't spending their time doing what they loved doing. They had lost their sense of purpose. They wanted to win so badly, but we just weren't."

Stengel started addressing those concerns one by one, and the effort had a real impact. For example, there had been a tradition at P&G whereby people would move to a new position about once every eighteen months. The practice wasn't very popular because it meant people had little time to get comfortable in their roles. Nonetheless, no one wanted to complain about it because it might seem that they weren't team players or didn't want to get ahead. But Stengel agreed that it wasn't the best way to utilize people's abilities, so he reframed the issue, stating publicly that he was going to keep people in their jobs longer in order for them to better develop their expertise. He also wanted to bring back a spirit of fun and creativity to the workplace, so he did things like take a group to the Cannes International Advertising Festival to show that he believed creativity was important. It was only after Stengel started to solve the problems that people were having and to change their perceptions about their work environment that things started to turn around financially as well.

Because I know it works, I believe it's absolutely imperative that you use an insight-driven approach like this, and believe me, I use it every single time I need to take people with me. As I've been writing this book, for example, I've also been preparing for our annual, end-of-year investors meeting in New York, where we go through the financial state of the company and present our future outlook for tomorrow and beyond. I've been the CEO of Yum! Brands for over ten years now, and I'm proud to say they've been really good years for the company. Our stock has consistently outperformed the market, and it was up over 40 percent going into this meeting. But talking about the past isn't all that compelling for investors; in fact, they think of past results as yesterday's newspaper. What investors want to know is whether we can keep the momentum going. Will we have another good year? Where will we be ten years from now? Have we run out of gas, or can we continue to grow? My challenge then became, how can we reframe our message, our performance, and our potential to investors in a way that addresses, head-on, how they're thinking at that moment? As you'll see in a few pages, that's exactly what we did. Getting inside the head of those you need is your starting place for taking people with you.

* What's Your Big Goal?

The first job of a successful leader is to have an idea of where you want to lead people. I start off my Taking People with You program with a straightforward question: *What's the single biggest thing you can imagine that will grow your business or change your life?*

I said it was a straightforward question; I didn't say it was an easy one. The answer that you come up with is what I call a Big Goal, by which I mean something more than just small improvements or modest growth. It's not very bold to do just marginally better than the year before.

Setting the right goal is the key to achieving success, and leaders often fall short in this area by not aiming high enough. None of us wants to fail, for a whole host of reasons (job preservation being among the top ones), so we tend to be cautious about how high we set our sights. But the truth of the matter is, shooting for just good enough rather than for greatness will not inspire the people around you. It also means you'll never get a chance to find out what you and the people you lead are truly capable of. And that's a shame, for your business, for your people, and for yourself.

So when you answer that question, take a moment to ask yourself: Am I thinking big enough? Use the following tool to help you think through your Big Goal and determine if you should be setting the bar a bit higher.

tool: picture step-change

Throughout this book, you will find tools like this one, which I learned from John O'Keeffe, who I mentioned in the introduction. These tools are intended to help you put important ideas into practice by prompting you to think them through and apply them to your own skills as a leader or to the goal you're trying to accomplish.

I use this tool, for example, to help ensure that I'm thinking *big* when setting goals for myself and my team. Imagine, for a moment, that you are a high jumper trying to figure out how high you should set the bar for your next jump. Should you set it a little bit higher than your last one? In order to make it over, should you use the same method you used before and just try a little bit harder?

What about a step-change instead?

How would you get over a bar that was set twice as high as your previous jump? You certainly wouldn't be able to jump that high using only your legs, so you'd have to think of new methods. You might use a vault pole, trampoline, or ladder to help you get over. Or maybe you could find a way to fly over the bar, in a hang glider, for instance.

Aiming for small improvements to the way you already do something is not going to change the way you think and therefore will not open up your mind to new possibilities. When you picture step-change, you are forced to come up with new methods with more potential.

Remember, it is easier to make powerful ideas practical than it is to make pedestrian ideas powerful.

Picture Step-Change for Your Business

A step-change or Big Goal, as I called it earlier in this chapter, is the opposite of an incremental goal. If your sales growth last year was 3.5 percent and this year you're aiming for 4 percent, that's incremental thinking. You have a good chance of reaching your target, but you'll never know how much better you could have done if you'd tried.

If instead your target is 15 percent, that's a bold challenge to set for yourself. Maybe you'll get there, maybe you won't, but making the attempt will get you further than if you hadn't tried at all. Suppose you only make it halfway to your goal: That's still a 7.5 percent increase, versus the 4 percent you were originally aiming for . . . a significant difference.

This tool works because the ideas you or your team come up with are linked directly to the size of the goal you put forth. Picture step-change first and then see what ideas you can come up with to achieve it.

Ways to Use This Tool

• Think about a current target. Now double it. What ideas spring to mind about what you would have to do to double it?

• Think about a current timeline. Now cut that timeline in half. What ideas spring to mind about what you could do to halve the timeline?

The ideas you come up with will be powerful, but it may take some work to make them practical. However, remember that it's easier to make powerful ideas practical than it is to make pedestrian ideas powerful. To bring this point home, when I was president of KFC, we had an average customer purchase cycle of once every fifty days. Rather than declaring war on our competition, I reframed our challenge, declaring war on that fifty-day cycle and making our step-change goal to envision feeding America a great tasting meal at least once a week. What would it take to do that? We knew we'd have to offer more variety than just fried chicken to get people coming back more often. As a result, we came up with some really successful new products that broadened our appeal, like our tender roast chicken for a non-fried option, crispy strips for a portable option, and pot pies as a home meal replacement. Getting our customers to come back every week was always aspirational, but that way of thinking helped us bring our customers in more frequently, shaving a couple of days off our average purchase cycle, which was a big win for us financially.

© John O'Keeffe, BusinessBeyondtheBox.com

✳ Who Is the Target Audience for Your Big Goal?

Can you achieve your Big Goal all by yourself? The answer is no. So *who do you need to affect, influence, or take with you to be successful?*

The answer to this second key question will establish the target audience for your goal. It may include your boss, your coworkers, people on your team, people from other departments whose help you'll need, or even people from outside your organization, such as shareholders, vendors, customers, or business partners. One of the biggest mistakes leaders make in this area is not thinking through *all* the people they have to lead to get where they want to go. You must do this in the same focused way that a marketer does when trying to identify potential customers.

The following People Map exercise will help you think through whom you need to reach to accomplish your Big Goal. We will come back to this map later in the book to make sure you've thought through everyone you need to take with you.

* People Map Work Sheet

As you think about what you want to accomplish, identify the people you need to bring with you to achieve your Big Goal.

1. Using the map below, write your Big Goal in the center circle.

2. Identify the groups of people you need to bring with you to achieve your Big Goal, such as your team, stakeholders, customers, etc. Think broadly: Are other functions involved? Other companies? Other industries? Have you considered everyone you need to bring with you? Have you looked up, down, and sideways across the organization?

3. Where appropriate, write the names of specific people within each group that you need to bring with you.

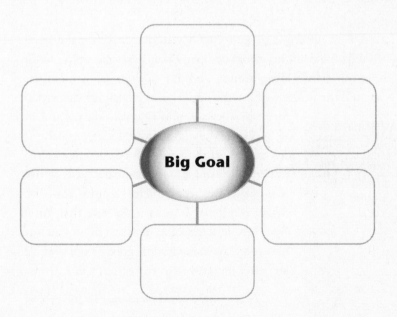

* What Is Your Target Audience Thinking?

Once you have a good idea of who you need to lead, the issue then becomes, how do you motivate them? The question to ask yourself here is the same one I used to ask as a marketer when selling customers on a new idea or product: *What perceptions, habits, or beliefs of my target audience do I need to build, change, or reinforce to reach my goal?*

Consider what their objections will be. It might be that your idea has already been tried and failed and they'll be thinking "been there, done that." If that's the case, you're going to have to overcome the belief that the idea is dead on arrival by making it clear why things can be different this time around. Or maybe your Big Goal will seem like a lot of work for your target audience without a lot of payoff. That's a perception you're going to have to address by showing people what's in it for them.

During the recent task of preparing for my investors meeting, I used this same process and answered all three of these questions for myself:

1. *What's my single biggest thing?* My Big Goal is to make Yum! Brands the defining global company that feeds the world. With our powerful global brands and 1.4 million team members around the world, we have the opportunity to define what makes for a best-in-class, multinational company and, in so doing, help make the world a better place. If we can do all that, we will be the envy of the restaurant business and a company others strive to emulate. But to get there, we must continue to get results. I want to make sure that Yum! Brands is on a trajectory for growth, so that our next ten years are at least as good, if not a whole lot better than my first ten years as CEO.

> *Leadership is the art of getting someone to do something you want done because he wants to do it.*
> —DWIGHT D. EISENHOWER

2. *Who do I need to take with me?* In the case of our annual investors meeting, the answer is our

existing shareholders, potential new shareholders, and the sell-side analysts, the experts who write the analyst reports that tell investors to buy, hold, or sell your stock. I realize that in order to meet my goal, I first have to convince people that it's possible. Without the faith of the investment community, it just won't happen.

3. *What are they thinking?* Here's where I asked my outstanding investor relations leader, Tim Jerzyk, what he'd been hearing from our target audience. He told me the biggest concern has been whether our company has hit its limit for growth and therefore whether it's the right time to buy our stock, given all our success. This is the perception problem that we've been up against, and we have to answer it.

To counteract this notion, the first thing I wanted to reinforce for investors was that we have a track record for driving results year after year. Here's where I pointed out that we've generated at least 13 percent earnings-per-share growth for each of the last nine years. This gives us credibility and gives investors a basis to believe that we will do what we say.

We wanted to change the perception that we may not be able to keep it going, so we elected to emphasize for investors the segment of our business that is growing the fastest: our international business. The focus of our presentation was "On the Ground Floor of Global Growth" and we found exciting ways to show that even though our restaurant brands are already thriving in global markets like China, India, and Russia, we have just hit the tip of the iceberg. China, which is a hugely profitable segment of our business, currently has just 3 restaurants per million people. Compare that to 60 restaurants per million in the United States, then factor in the growing population in China and their rapidly expanding middle class, and you can see that the growth potential there is enormous. We also talked about the potential for expanding in emerging markets like Southeast Asia and Africa.

We currently have a strong presence in both these areas, arguably the strongest foothold of any quick-service brand in existence, and there are ample opportunities to build from there. KFC is thriving in South Africa, for example, where in 2010 it was rated the third most-loved brand in the entire country, and the most popular retail brand of all. From that starting point, we are just beginning to branch out into new countries in Africa, like Nigeria, Ghana, Angola and Zambia. Many of these countries have stronger and more stable economies than people realize and are practically without competition in our category.

We showed investors the data, we laid out our plans, and by the end of the meeting it was clear we'd made a good start on taking the people in that room with us. This was verified by all of the positive analyst reports published the next day, which reflected confidence in our ability to grow over both the short and long term . . . just what we wanted to hear from our target audience.

The bottom line is this: If you can accurately identify the people you need to make something happen and then get inside their heads, then you will have the best chance of convincing them to help you accomplish big things. This may seem like common sense, but the thing I've realized about common sense is, it's not all that common. Too many people simply overlook this essential leadership ingredient.

So let's go to work on your initiative. Spend some time thinking about these three questions and filling out the following work sheet. The answers to these questions are your starting place. The goal you decide upon in this first chapter is the one this book will help you reach by showing you how to take people with you. What follows is a road map for making it happen.

go slow to go fast

David Cote, CEO of Honeywell International, started his career as an hourly employee, so he thought back to those days when trying to understand what his target audience, his plant workers, were thinking when management decided they wanted to introduce a new operating system. "Having been an hourly employee, I know there is a strong tendency to just be viewed as a pair of hands and not really engage people in thinking. So what we're doing is starting to engage our forty thousand [hourly employees] in that thinking process. And it takes time. You don't go to somebody who's been working in a factory for twenty years and tell them, 'Through Tuesday, you just keep doing what you're doing; Wednesday, we're starting this new program, so you need to start thinking completely differently.' There's a maturation process that you have to go through. So for us to actually convert a plant to a Honeywell Operating Plant—it takes two years. Because it starts with leadership, it starts with discussions, it starts with engagement. Sometimes you have to go slow to go fast."

* Big Goal Work Sheet

What Is Your Single Biggest Thing?

The single biggest thing you're working on *must* be step-change. It's not something you can easily accomplish in the next few days, weeks, or even months.

1. What's the single biggest thing you can imagine that will grow your business or change your life?

2. Describe the outcome you envision if you accomplish your Big Goal. As you write it down, ask yourself: Am I thinking big enough? Does this challenge get me excited? Does it make me a little nervous? Would my peers think it's not just a goal, but a Big Goal?

Who Do You Need to Bring with You?

Who is your target audience? Who are the people you most need to bring with you in order to achieve your step-change goal? Complete the TPWY People Map Work Sheet to answer this question.

What Perceptions, Habits, and Beliefs Most Impact Your Challenge?

What perception, habit, or belief of your target audience do you need to build, change, or reinforce to reach your goal? It may be different for different groups or individuals.

part one

get your mind-set right

h aving your head screwed on right is the foundation for any success you will ultimately achieve. In fact, there is no question in my mind that before you can be effective as a leader, you have to think like a great one.

Your ability to reach your goals has as much to do with how you choose to see the world as it does with your level of education and intelligence. And this is totally within your control because your mind-set is up to you.

Some mind-sets are good and powerful; others are bad and limiting. Consider this scenario that John O'Keeffe shared with us:

Two shoe manufacturers arrive in a new country looking to expand their markets. The local people, however, are very different from the customers they sell to at home. In fact, they don't wear shoes at all, preferring instead to walk about barefoot in all kinds of weather, at all times of year.

The first shoe manufacturer assesses the situation and says, "There's no market here. These people don't wear shoes!"

The second one looks around and says, "There's a huge market here. Not a single person is wearing shoes!"

The difference here is as obvious as night and day. How you view a situation or task at hand can dramatically affect the actions you take. The chapters in this section will give you the keys to thinking in a more powerful way about yourself, the people around you, and the work you want to get done.

tool: choose powerful vs. limiting mind-sets

What is a mind-set? It's a prejudice, a bias, a fixed way of looking at things. We all have them, some good and powerful, some bad and limiting.

Limiting Mind-set

• "What works in China won't work here."

• "Corporate doesn't understand my market."

Powerful Mind-set

• "It's amazing that a Western idea worked in China, so it's bound to work here."

• "Corporate can be a huge help to my market."

The key, when applying this tool to your own way of thinking as a leader, is to remember that a mind-set is something you choose, not something that you leave up to chance.

To Use This Tool

• Start by silently recognizing the limiting mind-sets you see in others (colleagues, family, friends). Notice how often people have mind-sets that weaken their results (e.g., I can't do that, I always mess this up, You cannot do *x* in a recession, etc.). These mind-sets are beliefs that people hold to be true. However, you know they cannot be universally true, because *you* don't hold them, or not all the time.

• Next, realize you are no different. You also have a set of limiting mind-sets that you hardly realize are there, though others are likely to see them in you.

• Admit that your mind-set is a choice because if what you believe were really true, there would be no need to *believe* it.

• Now, make an effort to choose mind-sets that will help you, not limit you.

© John O'Keeffe, BusinessBeyondtheBox.com

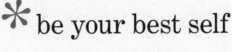

2 *be your best self

be yourself, know yourself, grow yourself

just be yourself.

I bet you've heard that advice many times before. I know I have. And I bet you've been told that, in business as in life, being yourself means being trustworthy and authentic and that if you don't come off as those two things, then you've failed already, because no one is going to follow you very far.

It's interesting how casually people often deliver this wisdom. They'll tell you to be yourself before a job interview or on a first date to help calm your nerves and take the pressure off. The implication is that you don't have to try so hard. Just relax. *Be yourself.*

Easier said than done. In reality, it's much harder to be yourself than most people are willing to admit.

Think about how often you've watched or listened to someone you don't even know that well, maybe a colleague or someone on television, and you could just tell that that person wasn't being authentic. During the 2008 presidential primary season in the United States, I remember watching the news on multiple occasions and shaking my head as the various candidates, trying hard to find their footing, flubbed in this regard over and over again. I remember a news clip of Barack Obama in Pennsylvania, where he was behind in the polls, donning bowling shoes and taking to the lanes in an attempt to connect with working-class voters. It was cringe-worthy watching him throw a pretty pathetic gutter ball, not so much because of his lack of skill, but because he looked so stiff and uncomfortable while he was doing it. By contrast, he was much more relaxed and relatable at a subsequent event where he played his favorite sport, basketball, with local voters. It was his game and you could just see it. And by the way, he's got a heck of a jump shot.

Around the same time, the press took Hillary Clinton to task for doing shots of whiskey and drinking mugs of beer at a bar in Indiana. The Web site Gawker, for one, mocked her for assuming the only way to appeal to blue collar voters was to drink "like a frat boy" (not to mention her choice of a *Canadian* whiskey). At a different event in New Hampshire, when a voter asked how she managed to keep on going day after day, she got choked up and responded, "It's not easy, and I couldn't do it if I just didn't passionately believe it was the right thing to do. I have so many opportunities from this country. I just don't want to see us fall backwards." This display of emotion struck people as genuine. After the clip was replayed in the media, she went up in the polls and went on to win the New Hampshire primary.

And lest you think I'm showing political bias with these examples, let's also pick on the Republican candidate, John McCain. The man was known as a "maverick" who stood up for what he believed in, sometimes even offending his own party in the process. But when he chose Sarah Palin as his running mate after it had been reported that he favored the independent senator Joe Lieberman, he lost some of his credibility. His attempts to convince Americans that she had been *his* choice and that he hadn't been pressured into it by members of his party just didn't ring true.

The point is this: These politicians are incredibly accomplished people. Plus, they have top advisers to help them create an image that will appeal to the public, yet they still get tripped up when they try to be something they're not. Being true to yourself is a daily challenge that's hard for everyone, no matter what your job title is.

* Extraordinary Authenticity

People know and follow the real deal when they see it, those who walk through life on their own terms, who stay true to their beliefs, and who don't back down. We can all name people like this, and there's often a pretty broad consensus that such diverse figures as Nelson Mandela, Mahatma Gandhi, Oprah Winfrey, Muhammad Ali, and Winston Churchill are (or were) all real deals, which goes to show that authenticity can be demonstrated in many different styles.

I call this having "extraordinary authenticity," which means having the ability to be yourself even in the toughest situations. This requires living with a paradox: To inspire as a leader, you need to know your stuff, but you also need to be able to admit when you don't know stuff. You need to be both confident and vulnerable at the same time. I struggled with that paradox myself when, in 1996, at the age of forty-three, I was given the job of president of KFC.

It was the first time I'd been the president of anything, and because it had been a career-long goal of mine to one day be in charge of running a business, I was excited to get started. I really wanted to be good at it, to have a positive impact on the brand and the people working with me, and I wanted to turn around what had been a business in decline and have some fun along the way. But like many people with the best of intentions, I learned the hard way what I wasn't good at. For example, for the life of me, I have never been able to tell a scripted joke.

Toward the end of my first year as president of KFC, I brought all of our company restaurant general managers, more than two thousand of them, to our headquarters in Louisville for a meeting. Business was improving, and I wanted to give us all a chance to celebrate the accomplishment and encourage everyone to continue in the right direction. As we were gearing up for the event, someone in my office came up with the idea of making a video to play on the bus ride from the hotel to our facilities, which would welcome the RGMs to Louisville and tell them what to expect in the days ahead.

The video, with me as narrator, started out with a spoof of the David

Letterman show, complete with an opening monologue and Letterman-style Top Ten List. When you see the video, you can tell I'm reading jokes off a teleprompter, and even though I wasn't on the bus while it was playing, I'm certain that the only laughs I got were from the laugh track the tech guys included on the tape.

I still cringe for that guy up there in the video when I watch it. He hardly seems like me at all. I'm not a formal guy, but I look so stiff. I've never been very good at reading off teleprompters, preferring good old-fashioned paper notes when I have to give a speech. The only part of the video that works is when I threw the script away and asked for some feathery chicken feet I knew we had in storage for special kid events. Then I just had fun being myself as I walked through the KFC headquarters talking to whomever I met along the way about everything from the history of Colonel Sanders to what we do in our research kitchen.

I've showed that video at my leadership seminars for years and it always gets a big laugh (at me, of course, not at my jokes). It certainly drives home the point about how easy it is to tell when someone isn't being themselves. But more important, when I show it, I let everyone know how much I still hate seeing myself bomb like that. Being yourself means letting your weaknesses show too.

Allowing yourself to be vulnerable can be hard enough for most of us, but in the business world, the idea of being yourself is further complicated by the fact that it's also important to get along with all sorts of people while staying true to yourself. You obviously can't just say to colleagues or customers, "This is me being myself, take it or leave it." Not if you want to get ahead. Instead, you have to figure out how to be you in a way that broadens your appeal and impact versus turning people off or unnecessarily clashing with company culture.

The CEO of PepsiCo, Indra Nooyi, really struggled with this when she first came to the United States from India early in her career. "There were many times that I felt like a fish out of water," she told me, "times that I said to myself, 'Do I even fit in?'"

Rather than completely change herself, Indra found ways to adapt that felt comfortable to her. One such way had to do with her lifelong love of cricket. No one in this country followed the game, but they did follow baseball, another bat-and-ball sport. So she threw herself into baseball and into the local team, the New York Yankees, reading everything she could on the subject until she could comfortably talk about it. "Once I did that," she said, "I could then say, 'I really like this game and I like the Yankees,' as opposed to pretending."

Nooyi could have learned about football or taken up golf in order to better fit in with her American colleagues, but that wouldn't have suited her personality or her interests. At the same time, she didn't just sit back and say, "I don't care about any of these silly American pastimes. If the guys around here want to get to know me, they can ask me about myself." Instead, she sought out ways to connect with people that suited both her and them. "Rather than completely change myself to be something I couldn't live with, on the margin I tried to adapt and fit in, but in a way that made me comfortable." It took work to figure out how to be herself in a new environment, but Indra did it in a way that was uniquely and authentically her.

mind-set check

Refer to the tool for choosing powerful versus limiting mind-sets on page 28. In each one of the chapters in this section, you will be asked to contemplate your mind-set in relation to the topic at hand. Ask yourself: Is my mind-set helping me be a better leader and get big things done? Or is it getting in the way of my success? Is there a more powerful way of thinking that I could adopt?

*"There is always room to grow and improve
and be a better me."*
versus
"I don't need to change. I'm good enough just as I am."

* Know Yourself

Part of what's hard about being ourselves is we don't always know exactly who we are, especially early in our careers. It takes time and experience to develop the confidence and knowledge you need to do this successfully.

Early in my career, I worked with a lot of accomplished people with MBAs from Ivy League schools, whereas I had only a bachelor's degree, and it wasn't even in business; it was in journalism from the University of Missouri. I was different and I knew it, but it took a while before I had the confidence to admit it. As silly as it may seem, for years when conversation turned toward the subject of where people had earned their MBAs, I'd excuse myself to go to the bathroom so I wouldn't have to answer the question.

Thankfully, I eventually realized that hiding wasn't going to get me what I wanted. Maybe I didn't have an MBA, but I was pretty good at seeking out the knowledge I needed to move ahead. When I was head of marketing at Pepsi-Cola Company, I went to the CEO, Craig Weatherup, and asked him to make me chief operating officer even though, up until that point in my career, I'd had absolutely no operating experience of any kind. I knew, however, that I didn't want to be a marketing guy my whole career and that if I wanted broader responsibilities, I needed broader experience. Craig and I got along pretty well, but I clearly wasn't the obvious choice, so I made him a deal: Test me out in the position, and if I failed, he

> *I had a lot of challenges getting comfortable in my own skin. When we went public, I was a terrible public speaker . . . so I certainly had to learn about that. When we started the business, I had never led anybody, but I had been on a lot of sports teams . . . I just sort of felt like, Well geez, if I can just make everybody feel like we're on the same team, we'll do well.*
>
> —BOB WALTER, CEO, CARDINAL HEALTH

could bump me back down to marketing, even fire me, whatever he thought was best. So he gave me a shot and neither one of us was ever sorry.

Self-awareness is a concept that will come up again and again throughout this book because you'll never get better at what you do without it. It's crucial for every great leader to know who they are and where they've been. The following exercise is an invitation to take a hard look at your past and think about the events that have most deeply shaped you, your values, and your goals. I've included my own lifeline as an example, and the events I mentioned above are included on it. I still look at and add to it from time to time to remind me of where I've been, what I've learned, and what lessons have not come easily to me. Knowledge doesn't spring out of nowhere, and this exercise will give you a better picture of who and what have helped you learn.

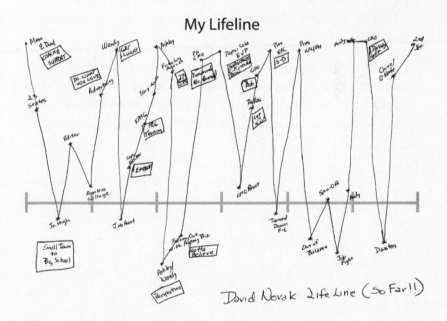

My Lifeline

✳ Lifeline Exercise: Get to Know Yourself

To be a better you, you need to understand who you are and how you got where you are today. Use this exercise as a chance to think about these things and get to know yourself a little better. Take some time with this, and consider including on your lifeline both personal and career events that have affected you in some way.

Directions

1. When plotting your lifeline, consider key events in your life, such as graduations, marriage, deaths, job chances, etc., as well as other experiences: victories you've achieved, crises you've endured, fears you've overcome, stands you've taken, and lessons you've learned.

2. Place points above and below the horizontal line to correspond with the intensity of emotions that accompanied each event or experience.

3. Once you feel satisfied that you've captured the events and experiences that have shaped you, draw a line connecting the dots. Feel free to add notes, draw pictures, or otherwise embellish your lifeline . . . anything that makes it feel more personal.

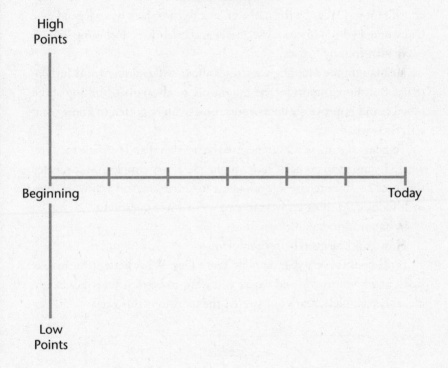

Your Lifeline

* Grow Yourself

I started out in the advertising business, and I did pretty well. In fact, at the tender age of twenty-seven, I was put in charge of one of the agency's biggest accounts, Frito-Lay.

Now, my boss at the time thought I was a little rough around the edges. Plus, I was a good ten years younger than the clients I was dealing with. He thought I needed a little polish, so he sent me to an image consultant in Dallas by the name of Jack Byrum. Jack was a legend who had worked with numerous executives and celebrities, including *Tonight Show* host Johnny Carson.

Jack taught me a lot of great things about self-awareness and authenticity. But more important, he taught me to always be thinking about how I could improve on these fronts. Once you've gotten to know yourself, then what?

To help take my self-awareness to the next level and help me focus on where I wanted to go next, Jack taught me a very simple exercise called the three-by-five exercise. He asked me to write down on a three-by-five-inch index card short answers to two very simple questions:

What am I today?

How can I be even better tomorrow?

I still do this every year on New Year's Day. What better time to take stock of where you are and where you want to be next year? For example, this past New Year's I answered the questions this way:

David Novak - 2011

What am I today? | How can I be even better tomorrow?

- Passionate/Convicted → Don't overwhelm/intimidate others
- Creative → Stay _focused_ until job is _done_!
- Instinctive → Balance with facts/process and discipline
- Driven for Results → Instill even more urgency:
  So What / Now What !!!
- Striving for Balance → More time at home / stay in shape

_DO IT_ !!!

To give you a better idea of how this can work, I'll explain a couple parts of this example. For one thing, I'm naturally a very passionate person, which is a useful trait for a leader, good for keeping people motivated and rallying their spirits. But that, combined with my positional power and the fact that I have strong convictions, can sometimes intimidate others, especially team members who don't know me very well. So I need to do everything I can to make sure I encourage other points of view by asking people who are not forthcoming to speak their minds.

I'm also a creative thinker who loves nothing more than coming up with new ideas. That may sound like a good thing, but it can be particularly dangerous when I find myself with a day when I don't have a lot to do. On days like that, some people would take the opportunity to relax. But not me. Left to my own devices, I start dreaming up more stuff the organization can do before we've finished the things we're currently working on. And that's not good. It means creating activity instead of action. But because I know that about myself, I can work on it. And that's exactly what I've been doing this year.

3 × 5 exercise: grow yourself

This simple exercise uses a 3 × 5 card to answer two questions: the first one about where you are in your career or personal development today, and the second about where you want to be in the future.

I encourage you to do this exercise now in the space provided and also to make a point of doing it regularly for the rest of your career. All you need is a 3 × 5 card and a little time to reflect.

What Am I Today?

Write down 4 or 5 descriptors that best capture how you are perceived by others today. Be honest with yourself. Think about feedback you have received from others or insights you have previously discovered about yourself.

Perceived Today	More Effective

How Can I Be Even More Effective Tomorrow?

Now write down how you can be better: How can you leverage your strengths even more? Or how can you adjust or compensate for those less-than-powerful areas? Once you've completed this exercise, refer to your card often to build your intentionality toward making it happen. I had my own 3 × 5 card laminated and taped to my office desk where I can see it every day.

* Be Your Own Masterpiece: Be Your Best Self

The best leaders understand that this is a lifelong process, that even if you make it to the top, you can never stop working on yourself. You have to continue getting to know who you are as a leader and how you can grow and improve.

Warren Buffett is one of the realest deals I know. I love learning from him. In fact, I have a ritual with the world's most famous investor: Every year I have the privilege of taking him to lunch at a KFC in Omaha, Nebraska, where his company, Berkshire Hathaway, is headquartered, and we talk about whatever is on our minds.

At one of these lunches, while he was devouring our Original Recipe chicken, to which he likes to add a ton of extra salt, I asked him what he looks for when he acquires a company.

We cannot become what we need to be by remaining what we are.

—MAX DE PREE, AUTHOR AND FORMER CEO OF HERMAN MILLER

"I'm looking to buy companies that are run by painters who are working on a painting that isn't finished yet. They know what the painting can be and they are passionate about making it as great as it can be."

I loved that analogy because it reminded me that business is always a work in progress. It also got me thinking about what makes a great painting. A great painting, a masterpiece, is a one-of-a-kind that's like nothing else on earth.

When you think about it, you're like that too. No one has your DNA. No one is like you. The best leaders are the ones who understand that they are like no one else, that they have a unique set of strengths and weaknesses, interests and knowledge, and that they are always going to be a work in progress.

* How to Be Yourself

I was talking about this subject in my Taking People with You program one time, and someone said to me, "Hey, it's easy for you to be yourself. You're the CEO. You can be whatever you want to be and people have to adjust to you. But how do *I* do it?" It was a good question. It's true that it's easier for me at this stage of my career, but I wasn't always the CEO. Looking back over my career, there have been numerous times when I wanted to get to the next level and I had to decide what I needed to do and who I needed to be to get there. I always fell back on the idea that I needed to be me and build on that, rather than trying to be someone I'm not. It's a good thing to think about as your career progresses. Here are

You were born an original. Don't die a copy.

—JOHN L. MASON, AUTHOR

some ways to help you be yourself no matter where you are in your career:

- *Have Conviction:* Being yourself is the only way to be. Acknowledge that it's key to building trust and credibility with others.

- *Know Your Stuff:* There is no substitute for time and experience. Building your know-how will give you confidence.

- *Know Your Environment:* Being yourself does not mean ignoring the impact you're having on the people around you. Remember the example of Indra Nooyi: In business, you have to be yourself while also being compatible with your company's culture.

- *Build Self-Awareness:* Constantly solicit feedback so you know how you're impacting others. Ask people what they would do if they were in your position.

- *Be Open and Honest About What You Don't Know:* It's amazing how liberating it is to do this and how much more people will get behind you if you do. It builds trust and gives people a chance to contribute their own knowledge.

- *Use Positive Self-Talk and Positive Thought:* Reminding yourself of your strengths and your accomplishments will help you to believe that you can succeed. When the dragons of self-doubt come creeping in is a great time to look back at your lifeline to remember how far you've come while being careful not to get mired in negative things of the past. We all need to realize that our outlook on life affects how we act toward people and situations in our daily lives, so tune in to your thoughts and make them as positive as possible. Try it for yourself and you'll see: it's impossible to be thinking positive things and feeling negatively at the same time!

- *Get Out of Your Comfort Zone:* Use your unique gifts and keep pushing the boundaries of your potential. Mark Chu, now the president of Yum! China, started out as a McDonald's restaurant general manager. He's a dynamic and humorous speaker in his native language but barely spoke English when I first met him in 1997. Now he presents in English to our board of directors and can crack a joke with the best of them. You never know what you're capable of. By the way, the only Chinese I know is *ni-hao* (hi), *xie-xie* (thank you), and *duo-kai-yi-xie* (build more!).

Another thing people always ask me is, "How can you be yourself when you disagree with your boss?" to which I say, "Team together, team apart." By this I mean that when you're together with your team, always have the courage to express your point of view (team together). That's what teaming up is all about, and you'll be able to sleep better knowing you spoke up. If your boss decides to go a different route, support that decision (team apart). You gave it your best and were true to yourself, but you also need to accept that the boss is the boss. This way you demonstrate that you are an independent thinker who can also play team ball, which is key if you want to climb up the ladder in any organization.

* How to Help Others Be Themselves

As the leader, your responsibility doesn't end with just getting good at being you. You also have to communicate to everyone you lead how important it is for them to be themselves too. Here are some ideas that will help:

- *Believe in All People*: Celebrate individuality. Even though the personalities on your team may be very different, as long as everyone is working toward the same goals with a similar value system that reflects a respect for others and a sense of personal accountability, that's OK. I call this "unity of values, diversity of styles." Allow the people you lead to succeed in their own ways, not as carbon copies of you.

- *Provide Individual Development Plans*: There's no substitute for tailored, constructive feedback. Express your appreciation for people's strengths and take the time to understand what makes them tick. Then help them identify ways to be even more effective.

- *Create a Safe Haven:* Make it easy for people to speak up, share their points of view, and express their individuality. Allow people to disagree with you, and when they do, thank them for it.

- *Openly Seek Knowledge and Perspective from Others:* Don't wait for people to speak up. Ask them what they know and what they think about your ideas.

* Insights and Actions

When doing the self-reflections and exercises that end each chapter, think about how those you lead would characterize your leadership skills. Solicit opinions from colleagues or people on your team if necessary. Even if you think you're pretty good in a particular area, try to think of some ways you could be even better. We're aiming for breakthrough results here, which means that pretty good isn't good enough.

These questions are designed to help you pinpoint your strengths and weaknesses and determine what you can do next to be an even better leader so that you are better prepared to accomplish your Big Goal.

Self-reflection

Assess yourself on the following items related to Being Your Best Self:	Personal Opportunity	Personal Strength
1. I never pretend to be something I'm not.		
2. I am aware of my strengths and weaknesses as a leader.		
3. I make my values and principles clear to those around me every day.		
4. Others view my behavior as predictable, reliable, and consistent.		
5. I am continually working on being the most effective leader I can be.		

Exercises

Look back at your lifeline and answer the following questions:

1. What experiences on your lifeline have most affected the way you lead people today? What did you learn from each experience?

2. Who were the people who have had the greatest impact on your lifeline? Who has led you?

3. What qualities do you admire most about the leaders who have most affected you? What steps could you take to be more like them while being true to yourself?

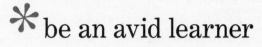

3

*be an avid learner

seek and build know-how

One of the most effective things you can do to continue to grow and be your best self is to always be learning. In fact, I believe that being an avid learner is the single biggest thing that separates a good leader from a great one. Someone with a voracious appetite for knowledge is bound to inspire others with their passion and curiosity and can energize an organization by bringing to it new ideas.

I've never taken an IQ test, but I know there are a whole lot of people out there who are smarter than I am. Still, I've managed to do pretty well in my career, and I'm certain that what separates me from others is that I always make an effort to prioritize knowledge and ideas over ego and ownership. Why is this so important? Well, obviously the more I know about a problem, the more likely I am to make a good decision. But even more important than that, being able to admit up front that I don't have all the answers helps establish an atmosphere in which the people I lead are more willing to share what they think and what they know. And if all members of your team are actively learning all they can about a problem and freely sharing their wisdom with you and with each other, then that's the best chance you've got of coming up with a solution that makes your business a whole lot better.

I will take good ideas wherever I can find them. In fact, some of the biggest successes of my career have been the result of building on the ideas of others, and I'm not too proud to admit that some of those ideas came directly from competitors. For example, when I went to Pizza Hut to run marketing in 1986, sales were down, and the brand hadn't had any successful new products in years. One of the emerging concepts in the industry back then was specialty pizzas, and one of the places that was doing that better than anyone else was California Pizza Kitchen. They excelled at using known flavor combinations to make unique specialty pizzas, like barbecue chicken pizza, Thai chicken pizza, and BLT pizza.

So one day I took my team to Los Angeles, and we went to CPK for lunch. We ordered practically every specialty pizza on the menu and really enjoyed them. It was clear they were on to something, but we weren't CPK. Could we make this concept work at Pizza Hut without losing what makes Pizza Hut unique?

Pizza Hut was then and still is more mainstream than California Pizza Kitchen, so the answer wasn't as obvious as having a Pizza Hut version of their Thai chicken pizza. At first, we tried a Cajun pizza, but that didn't really hit a home run with our customers. They wanted new menu options, but they didn't really want strange new flavor combinations. Next we decided on a specialty pizza that gave our customers more of what they already loved. First up was a Meat Lover's Pizza, which was such a hit that it led to our Cheese Lover's Pizza and then to a whole new "Lover's" line that has become a phenomenal success. Our Pepperoni Lover's Pizza, which is just a regular pizza with an extra helping of pepperoni on top, was one of the most successful new products in Pizza Hut history.

✳ 1 + 1 = 3

This kind of pattern thinking, where you look at what's working for someone else and apply it to your own situation, is one of the best ways to make big things happen for you and your team. Combining the knowledge of others with what you know about your own brand and industry can lead to results that are more than just incremental improvements; they can help you take a giant leap forward. The whole can actually be greater than the sum of its parts.

Another example of this happened early in my career when I was head of the Frito-Lay account at my ad agency. One day I decided to take my team to the grocery store to look around and get some ideas. That might not come as a surprise, considering the fact that Frito-Lay products are sold in grocery stores all over the country. What was surprising was how much time we spent, not by the snack foods, but in the salad dressing aisle.

The Frito-Lay account included Doritos, which at the time had only one very popular flavor, Nacho Cheese Doritos. But while perusing that salad dressing aisle, we made a discovery: Ranch dressing was far and away the best seller in the category at the time. That gave my team and me an idea: Would ranch dressing work as a chip flavor?

We went to Frito-Lay with the concept, but then it became a matter of how to position the product. So I looked at what had worked for Nacho Cheese Doritos. They had applied a unique image—nacho—to a known quantity—cheese—to make a product that was both exciting and appealing at the same time. So I asked, "How can we do the same thing for our ranch-dressing-flavored tortilla chip? How can we give a bit of uniqueness to the known quantity, which was ranch dressing?" That eventually led to Cool Ranch Doritos, which was not just a hit, it was a megahit. It's now one of Frito-Lay's biggest-selling and most profitable products.

This kind of pattern thinking requires that you keep your eyes open and actively seek out new ideas wherever you can find them. And you won't truly have your eyes open unless you have enough humility to admit that the best ideas aren't always going to come from you. Sir Isaac Newton once said, "If I have seen further, it is by standing on the shoulders of giants." I love that quote and wholeheartedly agree, but I would go one more: You will see even further if you stand on the giants' shoulders and take pride in crediting and thanking them for the view.

mind-set check

"As the leader, I know the most."

versus

*"There is always more to learn, and everyone
I meet knows something I don't."*

* What Happens When You Don't?

This is really a matter of positioning yourself mentally so you don't miss opportunities simply because of pride or close-mindedness. Most of us have the best of intentions, and we don't mean to be this way, but every one of us is guilty of dismissing an idea simply because we didn't think it applied to our business or we didn't respect the source of the idea enough to fully consider it. The following are some of the things that might be happening in your business because you aren't as open as you could be to the wisdom of others:

You Blow a Big Idea: The biggest missed opportunity of my career came from dismissing too quickly the wisdom of those around me. When I was working at Pepsi, the biggest new thing in the beverage category was water. Clearly Canadian's flavored waters were among the hottest new products around. I was sitting in my office one day, thinking about all this, when I came up with an idea that was probably the best idea I've ever come up with in my career; at least that's what I believed at the time.

> *I'm always searching for a certain kind of humility in our most senior leaders, people who don't think they know it all. . . . You're fighting arrogance and bureaucracy every day, and if you have people that act that way, then it's never good.*
>
> —JEFF IMMELT, CHAIRMAN AND CEO OF GE

The idea was to do a clear cola, a clear Pepsi. I called my boss, Roger Enrico, who was the CEO of Pepsi at the time, and he thought it was a pretty good idea too. We did focus groups and took it to test market, and the response was unbelievable. Dan Rather even highlighted the product as the lead story on the *CBS Evening News* after a hugely successful test launch in Colorado.

At this point, I was full steam ahead. I wanted to get the product on the market fast before Coke, or someone else, could rip us off. To add further pressure, I got it in my head that we needed to launch this product nationwide in time for the next Super Bowl, so we could promote it during one of the biggest events of the year.

It came time to get the bottlers involved, and when I presented the idea to the Pepsi-Cola Bottler Association Board, I was so confident, I thought they'd probably stand up and applaud by the end of the meeting. They did like the idea, but they had a concern. "David," they said, "there's a problem with this product. It doesn't taste enough like Pepsi."

They were right, but I brushed off the concern. It wasn't supposed to taste exactly like Pepsi. It was supposed to have a lighter cola flavor. It was supposed to appeal to a new demographic.

"Yeah," they said, "but you're calling it Crystal Pepsi. If you call it Pepsi, people will expect it to taste like Pepsi. You need to make it taste more like Pepsi."

Sometimes our best assets can also become our blind spots. When I look back, I now realize I never really listened to the criticism because I figured I was the marketing expert and they just didn't get it. I went ahead and launched the product anyway. And we did it so fast that we had a small quality control problem. The product tasted great in the lab but it had a bit of an aftertaste in certain markets.

Well, the problems with Crystal Pepsi became sort of legendary. *Saturday Night Live* did a skit in which they poured Crystal Pepsi onto a pile of mashed potatoes, implying that it tasted like gravy. *Time* magazine later did a story on the top one hundred marketing failures of the twentieth century. Crystal Pepsi was in the top ten.

Perhaps the most amazing part of the story is that I didn't get fired as a result of all this. The reason I didn't is because we actually made money on it. Everyone wanted to try it, and it was the first Pepsi product ever launched at a premium price. The bottlers treated it like a novelty product that wouldn't be around that long, and they were right. What kills me to this day is that I still believe it was a good idea. If I had just listened to the people telling me that the product wasn't right yet, Crystal Pepsi might still be on store shelves as a big-selling brand. If we had just worked out the problems with the flavor quality in our plants. . . . If we had just built in a few more notes of Pepsi-Cola flavor. . . . If I would have just slowed down and not been such a heat-seeking missile . . .

It was the biggest missed opportunity of my career, and after that miscue, I never wanted to be left wondering "what if" again.

You're Late to the Table: Tom Ryan, recently retired chairman and CEO of CVS-Caremark, openly shares a great story about the importance of learning the difference between listening to be polite and truly listening for information. He thought he had listened when, in the early 1990s, people in his organization wanted to start a program of pharmacy drive-throughs so that customers could pick up their prescriptions without leaving their cars. Two of their competitors had had some success with the concept, but initially Ryan thought it was a terrible idea.

Ryan envisioned traffic jams outside stores. He was concerned that drive-throughs would make customers think of fast-food restaurants rather than pharmacies. He was so sure he was right, he didn't really hear what his people were telling him about how a lot of their customers had been asking for more speed and convenience. Eventually the success his competitors were having with their drive-throughs changed his mind.

> *Who would you want on your team more? The person who develops the half-baked idea that may or may not be a great hit, or the person who's gone out and found a great idea that's already worked, and then uses the knowledge they have of the environment in which they're operating to make the idea even bigger and better?*
>
> —ROGER EATON, CEO OF KFC

Today 30 percent of CVS prescriptions are picked up at the drive-through, with no loss to front-end sales, and Ryan can't help but regret that he didn't get onboard sooner. "I was so wrong, but I had this conviction!" he told me with the kind of humility experience brings.

You Waste Resources: A few years ago, Taco Bell was looking to get into the breakfast business. Other quick-service brands had done well in this area, and Taco Bell wanted a piece of it.

The concept the company first developed seemed to fit perfectly with the Taco Bell brand. "Breakfast that wakes you up" integrated Mexican-inspired flavors into breakfast products, like the fiesta salsa, zesty sausage, and bacon grilled stuffed burrito. In hindsight, the commercial created to advertise the new breakfast menu perfectly summed up the problem. It featured a scruffy-looking young guy on a subway during a morning commute. He danced around the train, singing to bleary-eyed riders about spicy new breakfast flavors, while backed by a squealing rock guitar. Unfortunately, it doesn't make you think "breakfast." Instead it makes you think, "Who the heck would want to deal with that guy first thing in the morning? He's scaring people!"

The thing was, Taco Bell's new breakfast products were scaring people too. After a highly disappointing test run (thirty days of advertising and people were only trickling into the restaurants), the team had to figure out what was going wrong. The answer? Customers didn't want a lot of "zesty" in the morning. They weren't looking for a rock 'n' roll breakfast. They wanted to ease into their days with minimal excitement, and Taco Bell was offering the exact opposite of that.

The frustrating part was that Taco Bell had tested breakfast once before and come to a similar conclusion. What's more, KFC in the United Kingdom had also tried to launch a new breakfast menu and encountered a similar problem: They developed a "hungry man" breakfast concept that was more in tune with KFC's full sit-down meal image than it was with what customers wanted for breakfast, which was something light and portable. But somehow the Yum! organization didn't share information well enough to learn from these past experiences. We didn't look hard enough at what had worked for our competitors in the breakfast category and what hadn't worked for us in prior attempts. We didn't listen hard enough to our customers who were telling us, pretty consistently, what they wanted. So Taco Bell basically had to start all over again when it came to breakfast and rethink its concept to broaden the appeal. Now, instead of excitement for breakfast, we have partnered with well-known and approachable brands like Seattle's Best Coffee, Johnsonville Sausage, Quaker, and Cinnabon. And instead of focusing on spicy ingredients, we've appealed to customers by offering them value with our "Why Pay More for Breakfast!" campaign. This time around, we're having much more success, and so is KFC, now that we've modified our products based on these lessons.

* What Happens When You Do?

When faced with trying to accomplish a Big Goal, one of the most daunting questions is: Where do I start? "Standing on the shoulders of giants" is another way of saying you don't have to start from scratch and you don't need to reinvent the wheel. In business, we sometimes get too caught up in the idea that we need to be different, that we need to innovate. Of course we need to distinguish ourselves from our competition, but that does not mean we can't borrow good ideas, make them our own, and do an even better job of executing them. When we first spun off from PepsiCo, we had a tremendous opportunity. When my daughter, Ashley, was young and she made a mistake, she used to look at me and ask, "Dad, can I have a do-over?" That's where we were as a company. The restaurant businesses had been struggling, which was a major reason why PepsiCo leaders thought they'd do better if they spun us off. But in my mind, that gave us the opportunity for what I characterized as a "gigantic do-over."

To take advantage of our unique position of being a brand-new public company made up of well-established brands, we went out and did a best-practice tour of some of the most successful companies around at the time in order to take inspiration from them and borrow any good ideas we could find.

We visited seven companies in all—GE, Walmart, Home Depot,

Southwest Airlines, Target, Coke, and UPS—and then came back and crystallized what we'd learned into five things that we called our Dynasty Drivers, because these were the things that we believed would make us an enduringly great company:

1. *A culture where everyone makes a difference:* We saw this at Southwest, where they believed in "people first," and at Walmart, where we saw a big sign posted in one of their stores for all employees to see: TODAY'S STOCK PRICE IS ___. TOMORROW'S IS UP TO YOU.

2. *Customer and sales mania:* Home Depot was really a leader in this area. They had this concept of doing "whatever it takes" to build customer loyalty. To encourage accountability, they created an ownership culture, and every employee in their stores wore an apron sporting the message, I'M AN OWNER.

3. *Competitive brand differentiation:* At Target, leaders talked about the concept of exaggerating the differences. CEO Bob Ulrich told me a story about how their aisles were bigger than the competition's and every year someone would come in talking about how it would be more cost-effective to make the aisles smaller. To which he would reply, "But then we wouldn't be Target, we'd be like everyone else."

4. *Continuity in people and process:* At UPS we learned how they put processes and discipline around what mattered most to their business—their drivers. They had developed a whole science of how to make delivering packages easier and more efficient for the driver, from the comfort level of their seats to the height of the step going in and out of the truck. Every detail mattered. And we noticed that all the great companies had CEOs and functional leaders who had worked together for years so they knew their business cold.

5. *Consistency in results:* Coke and GE excelled in this area. At GE we learned about what Jack Welch called the "relentless

drumbeat of performance." These companies continually measured performance to make sure they were getting the results they wanted.

Just think about how much we advanced our position on the learning curve, in terms of what we needed to do to be a great company, by going out and studying those that were already great. One best-practices tour gave our company a base of knowledge and a focus that we have been building on ever since.

＊ Become a Know-how Junkie

That early best-practices tour really reinforced the idea in our company that, for any problem we need to solve, learning all we can about it is the best place to start. There is always more to know, and when people ask me what I look for when hiring someone, an avid learner tops the list. People who are avid learners love what they do and seek out know-how wherever they can find it, which makes them a whole lot smarter and their results a whole lot better.

The examples below are tangible benefits that have come about as a result of our companywide commitment to always be learning, to being "know-how junkies." They should give you some ideas about how you, as leader, can seek out opportunities for both you and your team to expand your knowledge about your business:

McDONALD'S IMMERSION DAY: Over the past six years, McDonald's has grown its average unit volume by 40 percent, which resulted in a dramatic turnaround of the brand. So a few years ago, I asked every leadership team we had around the world to go to school on McDonald's. We learned everything we could about them through store visits, research, and tapping former employees, which sparked our commitment to focus even more on the basics of operational excellence as well as to leverage our restaurants more throughout the day with the launch of breakfast menus and by expanding our beverage line beyond carbonated soft drinks.

BEST-PRACTICING APPLE: On the surface, Apple's business may seem very different from ours. Nevertheless, the CEO of Taco Bell, Greg Creed, and his senior leadership team visited Apple in 2010 because the company has had such phenomenal success with creating new products that people want and a brand image that people buy into. One of the things Apple leaders talked about was the idea of "addition by subtraction," which for them meant that, even though they could put forty buttons on an iPod, isn't it more appealing for the customer to have to deal with just a few? Everything for them comes back to clarity and simplicity, and those concepts have been applied by leaders at Taco Bell in a variety of ways. For example, the team launched a menu-simplification effort that reduced the number of food items offered in order to make it easier for customers to order while, at the same time, allowing us to improve our speed of service.

SHARING ON ICHING: We have such a big company and so much know-how within it that one of our biggest challenges has been to figure out how to share that knowledge efficiently and effectively. To figure out how we could make sharing easier, a team headed by our former chief operating officer, Emil Brolick, visited IBM, P&G, and Microsoft to find out about their systems for sharing knowledge. The result was iChing, our own internal network for connecting to each other and sharing ideas and knowledge no matter where we are around the globe. And the most amazing part is that the system has been so successful, that now companies are looking at us as a best-in-class example of sharing know-how. We've shared our story with companies like Kimberly-Clark, Marriott, Best Buy, and Disney, among many others.

Four Tactics for Being a Better Know-how Junkie

1. *Eliminate "Not Invented Here":* The phrase *not invented here* refers to an unwillingness to adopt something because it didn't originate with you. As leader, it's your job to make sure that nothing gets in the way of a good idea, no matter where it comes from.

2. *Act Like You Own the Place:* I don't mean that you should act like you own the place in terms of your ego, but more in terms of how you think about the business. If you owned the company where you work, you'd be concerned with all aspects of it. You wouldn't just think about your own role or your own department; you'd think about the total picture. Adopting this attitude will force you to look at and learn about more aspects of the business, which will give you a broader perspective. It will also demonstrate to others your potential for taking on more responsibility.

3. *Keep Your Big Goal Top-of-Mind:* In the information age, knowledge is everywhere, so you have to be strategic about it. Have you ever noticed that when you decide which car you want to buy, you suddenly see that car everywhere you go? Well, that's not because everyone has the same car;

Each year I just wanted to do better, and knowing that we can't stand still, at the end of every year I would take some topic about the game and research it. I might take rebounding or I might take zone defense or I might take the fast break. I would take all the books written by coaches who I thought excelled in that particular area and I'd read them all and take notes on them. About some things I would call coaches and try to get all the information I could. When Alcindor [later known as Kareem Abdul-Jabbar] came, I'd never had anyone approaching his size, so I started contacting Wilt Chamberlain and coaches that had had extra-tall players and talked to players personally to get all the information I could acquire from them in regards to working with an exceptionally tall and talented player. So I think that working on these things in the off-season kept me sharp. . . . It's what you learn after you know it all that counts.

—JOHN WOODEN, COACH OF UCLA'S BASKETBALL TEAM, WINNERS OF TEN NATIONAL CHAMPIONSHIPS it's because identifying what you want gives your brain a focus and a filter. You have to do the same for your Big Goal. Keep your antennae up and your Big Goal top-of-mind, and you will suddenly see ideas for how to reach it everywhere you look.

4. *Seek Out Knowledge Holders and Sources:* Be proactive about gaining knowledge by searching for expertise. Who knows something about what you're working on? Go talk to those people. You'd be amazed how many doors you can open just by telling people you'd like to learn from them. In addition, where can you find information about what you're working on? Go look up those sources, whether they are case studies, books, business magazines, or what have you.

✳ Wiping Out "Not Invented Here" All Around You

> *I got to be about forty years old and finally had to admit that I didn't do everything perfectly. That first admission was probably the hardest. . . . I need to recognize I don't always have the best ideas. Our people don't always have the best ideas. My company doesn't always have the best ideas. So I need to be looking everywhere.*
>
> —DAVID COTE, CEO OF HONEYWELL INTERNATIONAL

Being open to and on the lookout for good ideas yourself is only half the battle. You have to position yourself so that good ideas can come to you. That means creating an atmosphere in which the people around you feel comfortable speaking up and know that there is a benefit to doing so.

Early in my career, I had a boss who, every time I came to him with a new idea, would answer by saying, "That's funny, I'd been thinking the same thing." At first I thought it spooky how alike we were, but pretty soon, I caught on. As the big boss, he didn't want to admit he hadn't thought of something himself. And it wasn't just me. Around the office,

"I was thinking the same thing!" became a punch line that one of us would shout anytime anyone had an idea, no matter how trivial. ("I think I'll go get a glass of water" . . . "Well what do you know, I was thinking the same thing!") Not only did our boss's bad habit dampen our drive to come to him with ideas that could improve the business, but it also caused us to lose respect for him as a leader. After all, if he needed to steal our ideas, he must not have been very confident about his own.

In contrast, Howard Draft, head of Draftfcb, one of the world's largest communications agencies, once told me how, even though he's been in the business for more than thirty years, he often relies on the ideas and opinions of young people right out of college. In a recent meeting where a team was working on a creative strategy for a Kraft product, he was offering the group his viewpoint when "this young woman with a pierced nose and red hair looks up at me and goes, 'You're absolutely wrong and here's why you're wrong.' I was so proud of her I went over and hugged her."

Imagine the difference in working for these two guys: One won't even admit your ideas are your own; the other is hugging an employee in front of everyone because she had the guts to stick up for her opinion, which she backed up with knowledge. Who would you want to work for?

> *I think the best thing I can do to become a better leader is to keep an open mind to all different points of view, learn and listen to people of other industries, because I think our world is changing so much that first we've got to figure out lots of dots and then figure out how to connect the dots. We need to recognize that there isn't a book on how to run a $40 billion, now going to a $60 billion, corporation. You don't just take the book from the rack and read it and become a leader. You have to write the book as you go along. It's the listening and learning that really makes a difference.*
>
> —INDRA NOOYI, CEO OF PEPSICO

Tactics for Wiping Out "Not Invented Here"

If you want to take people with you and reach your goals more efficiently and effectively, you need to learn to see every person and every experience as an opportunity to expand your knowledge base. The tactics below will help you ensure that you are truly wiping out "not invented here":

1. *Model the behavior by being a know-how junkie yourself:* When I was in marketing, I read *Ad Age* every week cover to cover. In fact, anything that had anything at all to do with marketing, I was all over it, looking for ideas and knowledge about what was going on in the industry. If you want your people to be learners, you have to show them that you have a passion for learning too.

2. *Actively listen to and learn from others:* One of the best things I do every year is attend meetings of the American Society of Corporate Executives. This is a group of about thirty active CEOs who get together periodically. The price of admission is that each person has to give a ten-minute presentation on something they've learned in the last six months, followed by a Q&A with the other CEOs. This is a group of very smart and very accomplished people, but it's amazing how much we can all still learn. I'm always surprised by how much knowledge I gain by just listening closely to a group of smart people talk for a few hours.

3. *Create a culture of healthy debate/healthy decision:* This means you have to establish a safe environment where people can share and disagree without fear. We had a board meeting once where Javier Benito, the chief marketing officer of KFC, came in to talk about our new Krusher frozen beverages. He was touting the new U.S. formula, which is different from the one that had been successful internationally. I didn't think the U.S. version was half as good, and I told Javier so at the meeting. He then told me all the reasons why he thought I was wrong. We went back and forth like that for a while in front of the board of directors, who are my bosses. After the meeting, I went straight to Javier's office and told him how much I appreciated that he had expressed his point of view. I still thought he was wrong, of course, and I told him that, too, but more important was the fact that he had displayed the courage of his conviction and the kind of behavior we want in our company. So I thanked him for it.

4. *Celebrate using someone else's idea:* There is no idea people love more than their own, but the higher up you get, the more important it is to celebrate other people's ideas more. Doing so will create an environment where people will want to come to you with their ideas, not hold them back. That's why, every time I talk about our Achieving Breakthrough Results program, I make sure to give Sam Su credit for being the first to discover the tools from John O'Keeffe. As Robert Woodruff, the former president of Coca-Cola, once said, "There is no limit to what a man can do or how far he can go if he doesn't mind who gets the credit."

5. *Share what you know:* As I mentioned earlier, I visit Warren Buffett every year, and when people in my organization hear this, they're always curious. Warren is one of the most respected minds in business today, and people always want to know what he has to say. So after each visit, I share his wisdom with my team. I've even started picking one of our top leaders to bring with me to our lunch every year as a reward for superior performance. That way, they can learn directly from him as I do.

> *If I were to say, "Look, this is Steve's idea and I think it's a great idea," people instantly listen. If you say, "I've got a great idea," people are a little skeptical because everyone loves their own ideas. Taking the ideas of other people and championing them is the best way of getting things done.*
>
> —MICKY PANT, PRESIDENT OF GLOBAL BRANDING, YUM! BRANDS

* Insights and Actions

Self-reflection

Assess yourself on the following items related to chapter 3, "Be an Avid Learner":	Personal Opportunity	Personal Strength
1. People around me would say I am a good listener.		
2. I am open about and willing to admit when I don't have all the answers.		
3. I regularly cross boundaries to include those who are different from me in order to expand my thinking.		
4. I readily adopt and integrate ideas and knowledge from others . . . and publicly give them credit.		
5. I set expectations and hold my teams accountable for sharing know-how with others internally and across organization boundaries.		
6. I regularly expose my people to the best technologies, minds, practices, businesses, training, etc.		

Exercises

1. Consider your responses above: Are you doing all you can to build know-how and expand your IQ?

- What additional know-how could I use?

- Where and when am I going to get it?

- Am I listening with an open mind to the thoughts and ideas of others?

2. Do you seek out opportunities to build your know-how? Think about the people you interact with on a regular basis and ask yourself:

- Who are three people I know who might have some knowledge that would help me execute my Big Goal?

- Seek them out and go get your know-how!

- What are two things you can start doing tomorrow that would help wipe out "not invented here" among your team?

4 * unleash the power of people

i believe leadership is a privilege. I also believe deep down in my bones that all people, when given a choice, have an inherent desire to do the right thing, to contribute, and to make a positive difference through the work that they do. And I'm absolutely convinced that it's crucial to have this mind-set in order to get the most out of the people you work with. As a matter of fact, I believe that there is potential in every person, and as the leader, it's my job to unleash it.

To put it another way, if there are distrust and bad feelings among the people you work with, is it any wonder that business suffers? I've often told the story about how, when I became president of KFC, I inherited not only a business in decline, but a system that was full of animosity. For a whole host of reasons (not the least of which was a pending contract dispute) the company's leadership and the franchisees simply didn't like or trust each other. I may have been new to KFC, but I understood right off that none of us was going to be successful in an environment like that.

My first official act as president was to get together with my executive team and let them know things had to change. I told them that I understood how hard things had been. "But," I said, "I want you to know something, I love working with franchisees. And from now on we're going to trust our franchisees. Fighting isn't doing either side any good. We might have some bad franchisees, but most of them put their blood, sweat, and tears into growing the KFC business, and one thing

I know for sure is, they don't like losing any more than we do. So I don't want to hear anything bad about them."

Next I had to convince the franchisees that it was a new day, so I went out to all nine of their regional association meetings and asked what *they* would do if they were in charge. I broke them into groups, and each group had to come back and present its ideas. Then I just sat back and listened.

That was the beginning of a new relationship. And I truly believe that if I hadn't started things off this way, what came next would never have happened. The two things that are largely credited with turning around KFC during my time as president from 1994 to 1997 are the introductions of two popular new products: Crispy Strips and the Chicken Pot Pie. And both of these products came about only because we had a more open relationship with our franchisees. Crispy Strips started because a franchisee down in Arkansas created, on his own, a freshly prepared chicken strip that helped boost his business by 9 percent. When I heard about this, we took the first plane down to have a look. We not only loved his product, but he took us to his supplier, who worked with our R&D team to get enough supply so we could roll the product out across the United States.

Our Chicken Pot Pie also was a result of working closely with franchisees. I created what I called our Chef Council, composed of franchisees who had a passion for making great food. We'd start taste-testing new recipes at 9:00 A.M. and eat so much some of us had to take a nap in the afternoon! One of the Chef Council members came up with a recipe for a pot pie that started the ball rolling for another big success.

The thing is, this helped make my career. Crispy Strips and our Chicken Pot Pie hugely boosted sales and led to other new products that did the same. KFC started growing again and almost doubled profits in just three years. And I got the credit for turning around a brand that had been losing for a long time. That success earned me a reputation for leadership that put me in a position to eventually run Yum! Brands. If you ask the finance people what ignited the business, they will tell you it was the new products, but my answer would be that it was a triumph of human spirit. It all started with one simple decision: to trust franchisees. That opened the way for them to trust me and the corporation in return, and together we unleashed the power of our people to succeed.

mind-set check

"Give people an inch, and they'll take a mile."

versus

"Believe in people, and they'll believe in you in return."

∗ What Happens When You Put Your Faith in People?

The thing people don't realize about trusting others is how much it can expand the possibilities for success. The following are some examples of how the simple act of putting one's faith in people has led to big financial success:

They Do Things Even They Didn't Know They Could Do: Early in his career, David Cote, now CEO of Honeywell International, had a new job running a chemical factory when, just three weeks after he started, one of the manufacturing guys came to him and said, "We just found an air permitting problem, and we're going to have to shut down that operation for two weeks." Cote was still just getting his footing in his new position, and as he told me, "Other than a high school chemistry class, I'd never had anything to do with chemistry." So he had no idea how to solve the problem. What he did know, however, was that there was no way things could be shut down for that long. "So," Cote recalled, "all I told him was that I refused to accept that." Instead, Cote suggested he get everyone together in a room who might be able to help and, in twenty-four hours, he wanted an answer as to how they could make sure a two-week shutdown didn't happen while still complying with the air permits.

The manufacturing guy looked at Cote and told him it was impossible, but Cote stuck to his position. "I remember walking out of there thinking, *Oh man, I don't know what else to do,*" Cote said. "*I just hope I'm right that they can figure this thing out.*" The next day Cote arrived early, thinking of how to manage the shutdown, and found that his faith had not been misplaced. Not only had the team come up with a way to fix the problem that wouldn't require a shutdown, the new solution was going to cost them $200,000 less than their original plan. Even Cote was amazed. He said to me, "That really stuck with me, because it shows that teams don't always know everything that they're capable of."

They Become More Invested in Their Work: I met leadership expert Ken Blanchard in 2000 at a KFC franchisee meeting, where he talked about the importance of creating a people-first culture within an organization in order to bring the concept of customer focus to life. After all, you can reach your customers only through your people, so you better hire great ones, train them well, and empower them to satisfy your customers. I liked what he had to say so much that I invited him to come to speak at one of our top-management meetings in Louisville, where he told a story about how Ritz-Carlton trained its hotel employees to handle customer complaints and gave them a $2,000 discretionary fund that they could use to satisfy customers without having to get anyone's permission first. We liked the idea so much, we brought it to Yum! and developed what we called a Customer Mania training program, which taught front-of-house employees how to listen to customers, be empathetic to their issues, recover from mistakes, and exceed expectations within reason. It also included a policy whereby restaurant employees could use up to $10 to help resolve customer issues on the spot without having to call for a manager. It had a huge impact on team members, who felt respected and empowered, and in turn, on customers, who felt their issues were being handled better and faster. (Ken Blanchard was so taken with our approach to building a new company that he even wrote a book about us called *Customer Mania: It's Never Too Late to Build a Customer-Focused Company,* which was published in 2004!)

They Rise to the Occasion: Stephen Burke remembers with trepidation the time when he was first asked to go to Paris to be the president of Euro Disney. The park had been open for only six months, and it was "in terrible shape," as he described it to me. "We looked at the numbers and realized that if we didn't do something very dramatic," he explained, "not only were we going to lose half a billion dollars the first year, but it was going to get worse because interest was going to compound." It was clear that what they had wasn't working, and what they had was a lot of Americans who had been sent over from Orlando to build the park and staff it. They were essentially using the Orlando handbook to manage the park in Paris, so Steve and his team decided to send the Americans home. In their place, they gave big promotions to a lot of young Europeans and encouraged them to figure out how to run the park so that it would please their European customers. "That was the single smartest thing we did," Steve told me. "It completely changed the company and unleashed a lot of enthusiasm. The thing it really taught me is that if you have people who are really in touch with the customer, if you have people who are excited about what they do, give them the keys, because if you do, they'll do the right thing nine times out of ten."

✳ Establishing Trust with Your Team

If you can establish an environment where every single person feels that they are part of a team and have a chance to contribute, you've created a situation where people can do great things. To build an environment like this, you have to start with trust.

Reaching out to people and building relationships based on trust might seem like a natural idea, but how do you do it? This is not the sort of thing they typically teach in business school. Below are things you can do to show people that you believe in them and that you care.

1. *Know That People Want to Contribute:* Start with the right attitude: Realize that 99.9 percent of people come to work every day wanting to do good and try hard. So *you* have to go to work every

day thinking about your people that way and appreciating them for it, not looking to catch the 0.1 percent who want to mess things up or don't act in good faith. This isn't always easy, because we all worry about the possibility of someone taking advantage of us; we fear we'll look bad if they do. But you have to remember, you're the leader, so it starts with you. If you don't trust people, why should they trust you? I can tell you one thing for sure, I've never ever trusted someone who didn't trust me . . . and I guarantee you it goes both ways.

2. *Demonstrate That Everyone Counts:* It's been shown that the most successful companies have a culture where every single person feels valued. No matter what their position, they all know they have a chance to contribute and make a difference. Coach John Wooden told me he used to liken his team to a car. One star player may be like the powerful engine while others are more like the nuts that hold on the wheel. "But if we lose that wheel, how good is that engine?" he explained. "Everyone is important. Everyone must feel that they are needed. If you feel you are not needed, I think you're through."

I recently saw an example of this when I visited India. Our team there, led by general manager Niren Chaudhary, has made corporate social responsibility a real priority, setting as their mission to achieve "growth with heart." One of their initiatives is to have at least one KFC store in every major city run by team members who are hearing and speech impaired. I visited one such store in Bangalore where they greeted me by doing our Yum! cheer in sign language. I was amazed to see how the kitchen worked with a system of lights replacing the buzzers and bells that typically tell staff when food is ready. At the front of the house, there are special menus that customers can point to in order to communicate their orders. The restaurant even provides table tents that teach people basic sign language, which the customers love. Niren's ability to see the potential in every person and to provide a place where that potential can be utilized has been a huge success. That restaurant in Bangalore is ranked the second best out of 118 stores in India. What's more, it serves as an inspiration to the entire organization as to what people are capable of.

3. *The More They Know, The More They Care:* This was a principle I learned when visiting Walmart. One way to show people you trust in their abilities and intentions is to share with them what you know. No one understood this better than Sam Walton, the founder of Walmart. Early on, he established Saturday meetings, where he would gather people together for the sole purpose of sharing with them everything he knew about the business. Why bother? He once wrote the following, which I think explains it: "The more they know, the more they'll understand. The more they understand, the more they'll care. Once they care, there's no stopping them. If you don't trust your associates to know what's going on, they'll know you really don't consider them partners."

4. *Ask Questions That Promote Insight:* To find out more about who people are and what they think, one of my favorite questions to ask is, "What would you do if you had my job?"

Getting inside people's heads is important, so don't be easy on yourself. Don't ask questions of just the people you work with every day. I call this "going two deep." It means you don't get to know what just your boss is thinking, you get to know what your boss's boss is thinking. And you don't get to know just your direct reports. Spend some time with those who report to your direct reports. Extend this idea even further, to customers or clients or anyone who might have something to do with the goal you want to achieve. Have you shown them that you care by asking them what they think and getting to know them better?

5. *Take Responsive Action:* Once you've found out what people think, you've got to act on that and show that you've taken them into account. John Calipari, head basketball coach at the University of Kentucky, told me how, in 2009, he recruited top high school player John Wall to his team. It was soon clear that this

guy was about to go pro, and Calipari could see that the other team members were growing jealous of all the attention he was receiving. Calipari could have just let his star player be, but that would have destroyed the spirit of the group and the trust they needed to have in each other to be a great team. So he took action. He pulled Wall aside and said to him: "John, you are definitely the star of this team and you are definitely going pro. I want you to take as many of your teammates as you can with you. You need to help them be great too."

Wall took his coach's words to heart and set his sights on improving not only his own performance, but the performance of everyone around him. The power of all that collective talent was unleashed. When NBA draft day rolled around, Wall was the number-one pick, followed by four of his teammates—DeMarcus Cousins, Patrick Patterson, Eric Bledsoe, and Daniel Orton—all of whom were first-round picks as well. It was a historic feat. Never before had more than four first-round picks come from a single team, but that year the University of Kentucky had five.

exercise: get to know people

Don't overlook the simple things, such as the fact that you can't really trust someone you don't know. Getting to know people will not only make you feel more comfortable when you have to rely on them, but taking the time to do this also shows them that you care.

On the next page is a relationship-building exercise that I learned from John O'Keeffe, which you can use with anyone you might want to ask for help in achieving your Big Goal. The key thing to remember is that the stronger your relationship, the more you can ask of people.

First, ask the person the following three questions. Resist the urge to respond or comment on what he or she says. Instead, just listen and thank your partner for his or her answers:

1. Tell me something you think I don't know about you.

2. Tell me something you like about me.

3. Tell me something you think we have in common.

Next, give your partner a chance to ask you the same three questions.

Here's the secret: You're going to do three rounds of this. By the third round, you'll both be struggling for responses, but don't let yourselves off the hook. Being intentional about your responses really makes a difference. If you choose to give superficial responses, you will develop superficial relationships.

Another approach comes from team members at Google. When in a meeting with people who aren't familiar with one another, instead of simply asking everyone to introduce themselves, the leader says, "Tell people who you are, what you do, and the closest you ever came to being arrested." Besides getting everyone's attention, this question helps establish an atmosphere of fun and openness right off the bat.

tool: trust model

This model, which was adapted from *The Trust Equation* by Charles H. Green (Trusted Advisor Associates, LLC), lays out what makes a person a trusted individual. Take a look at the points below and consider how well you'd rate in each area on a daily basis.

$$\text{Trust} = \frac{C+R+O}{S}$$

Trust Builders

Credible in Your Words
• Do you tell the truth?

• When you don't know, do you say you don't know?

Reliable in Your Actions
• Do you deliver on commitments?
• Do you commit only to things that you plan to follow through on?

Open to Other Points of View
• Do you actively seek input from others?
• Do you show people how you've acted on their input?

Trust Destroyer

Self-orientation
• To what degree is the focus on you versus others?

It takes twenty years to build a reputation and five minutes to ruin it. If you think about that, you will do things differently.
—WARREN BUFFETT

* Triumph of the Human Spirit

As I mentioned earlier, I considered the turnaround at KFC not so much a business success as a triumph of the human spirit. It wasn't business principles that really made a difference in this situation; it was people principles. It was the idea that if we trusted each other, we could work together to make something happen that was bigger than our individual capabilities.

A couple years ago, I encountered a much more important and profound example of this when I was in Europe visiting some of our restaurants and decided to take a weekend trip to Normandy. I'm a bit of a history buff, and this trip had been on my "bucket list," so I was excited to see the sites where the major events of D-Day unfolded, which turned the tide of World War II. I'd always believed it was important to build trust with your people and show them you care, but it really hit home for me when my French tour guide told me this story:

One of the many tales of heroism and leadership from that day centered on a place called Pointe-du-Hoc. There, a three-hundred-foot-high cliff juts out into the English Channel where Allied ships gathered to launch an assault. At the top of the cliff, you can look down on both Utah Beach on the left and

> *Through the whole time period, we accelerated management. Instead of having weekly risk meetings, we had three a day. Instead of having twelve people there, [it was] bring whoever you've got to bring who knows the facts who can impart them very quickly. So it kind of changed all the rules right there. It doesn't matter who you are, where it is, here's the meeting, you've got something to say you come up. . . . People were working on weekends going through all the credits, all the accounts, all the companies that might be in trouble. . . . I tell you, it was a beautiful thing to behold.*
>
> —JAMIE DIMON, CEO, JPMORGAN CHASE, ON HOW HIS ORGANIZATION MADE IT THROUGH THE FINANCIAL CRISIS

Omaha Beach on the right. At the top of that cliff on D-Day, German guns were within range of thousands of troops being deposited on the beaches below.

The companies charged with securing Pointe-du-Hoc suffered heavy casualties as they exited their boats, made their way across the wet sand, and scaled the cliffs. From D Company, for example, only twenty out of seventy men were still in fighting form when they reached the top. But the amazing thing was, those who remained on their feet, despite all the chaos, were still able to focus on their objective. This was true even after many of their leaders had fallen. When captains were killed, lieutenants took over. When lieutenants went down, sergeants took over. When sergeants fell, privates stepped up (and they were the ones who really won the battle). And so it went until they finished what they'd come to do.

Many things did not go as planned that day, but still the ultimate goal was reached: Allied troops got the foothold they needed on the western front. One of the reasons behind this success was General Eisenhower, who was in charge of the operation. Eisenhower allowed his people on the ground to make their own decisions in the heat of battle. He didn't try to micromanage; he simply trusted his people and his preparations and then waited at headquarters for news.

Before sending troops into battle, however, Eisenhower relayed to his officers a message that must have sunk in at all levels: "This operation is not being planned with any alternatives. This operation is planned as a victory, and that's the way it's going to be. We're going down there, and we're throwing everything we have into it, and we're going to make it a success." The taking of Pointe-du-Hoc is just one example—and there are many, many more—of how that message spread all the way to the men on the front line who threw everything they had into making their part of the operation a success.

By contrast, when Allied forces landed on D-Day, Hitler was asleep. That's not surprising considering the assault started around five thirty in the morning. What did surprise me—left me floored, in fact—was that, even though reinforcements were urgently needed, two of Hitler's panzer divisions remained immobilized for hours. You see, they could only be moved if the Fuhrer himself gave the order (he trusted no one else to do it), and none of his people had the guts to risk waking him up. The leader finally arose on his own around noon, and only then were his troops able to change their position. And to put that timing into perspective, Pointe-du-Hoc was secured by those brave Rangers by 9:00 A.M.

✳ Let Others Hold You Accountable

You'll force yourself to be a better leader if you let people know they can call you on it when you're not living up to your position. Most people, however, are used to being held accountable by their leaders, not the other way around. In order to get people's honest opinion about your business and about your own performance, you're going to have to ask them for it.

Jamie Dimon, CEO of JPMorgan Chase, told me a story not long ago on this very subject. He was reading customer complaints one day, which he does periodically as a window into how the business is running, when he came across one from an elderly lady about their credit card protection program. Chase's credit card business was sending out these rebate offers to customers, but as the fine print explained, when you returned the form to get your $9 rebate, you were also signing up for their protection program at an additional cost. This woman hadn't realized what she was signing up for and she wanted out. Jamie agreed with her, so he asked his assistant to get the credit department on the line, to which she responded, "Oh, we get tons of these." Jamie asked her why she hadn't mentioned it before, and she told him she didn't know that he wanted to hear that kind of thing from her. As Jamie told me, "I adore my assistant, but I said to her, 'Come on, if you think something is ridiculous, I want to know.' And she said to me, 'Well, that program is ridiculous.' I called the credit card people and got them to cancel it. As I told them, if you wouldn't treat your mother that way, don't do it." Like all good leaders, Jamie knows when you do right by the customers and people you serve, you always make more money in the end.

Right after becoming president of KFC, as I was wondering how I was going to handle the mess I had stepped into there, I stumbled upon a book that summed up the kind of leader I wanted to be. It was called

> *Trust helps you move quickly. It increases your speed. When it's absent, you can see it—more checks, controls, and processes. That's bureaucracy.*
>
> —RANDALL STEPHENSON, CHAIRMAN AND CEO, AT&T

Walk the Talk, and it talked about how leaders need to model the kind of good values they want their organization to live by, including the idea that each and every person in the company matters.

How often have you read a book, been affected by something in it, but then put it back on the shelf and largely forgotten about it? I didn't want that to happen to me. So to make sure it didn't, I gave *Walk the Talk* to every single person in our restaurant support center as a holiday gift and asked them all to hold me accountable to the principles within it. I did it to send a message: People are my priority. But I also did it for a very practical reason: As CEO, I have a lot of things I need to focus on, like our bottom line, the perception of our organization on Wall Street, and where the company needs to grow and improve. As leaders, it's easy to miss things because there are so many details we should be focused on. You'll do yourself a favor if you ask for help. As for me, I take all the help I can get.

✳ Insights and Actions

Self-reflection

Assess yourself on the following items related to chapter 4, "Unleash the Power of People":	Personal Opportunity	Personal Strength
1. I treat *all* members of my team in a way that makes them feel that they count and make a difference.		
2. I view others' mistakes as opportunities for learning rather than opportunities to criticize.		

Assess yourself on the following items related to chapter 4, "Unleash the Power of People":	Personal Opportunity	Personal Strength
3. I am very open about sharing information with all levels of my organization.		
4. I support my team's decisions rather than second-guessing or criticizing them.		
5. I ask probing questions to learn about my people, their ideas, and the business.		
6. I integrate others' ideas into plans and recognize them for their contributions.		

Exercise

Review your People Map from chapter 1 and ask yourself the questions below. Use different colors, additional paper, etc., as you update and make notes on your People Map to capture your thoughts and actions.

• Have you left anyone off your People Map? If so, add them!

• Trust is important, so rate the level of trust you have with the people on your People Map. How can you increase trust between you?

• Have you asked someone from every group for input on your Big Goal? Have you used their input or otherwise shown that you've listened? Have you recognized their contributions?

5 ✳ you have to believe it can be done

i n this section on mind-set, I really haven't focused much on the specific goal you set for yourself at the outset of the book. So far it's been more about how you think and view the world as a leader.

Now is the time to get back to the goal at hand. Think for a moment about what you want to accomplish, and ask yourself: Do you truly believe you can make it happen?

If the answer to that question is not an immediate and emphatic *yes,* then you have some work to do. In this chapter I'll talk about how to cultivate that can-do spirit in yourself and in those around you. It's crucial that this happens before you move on to the nuts and bolts of getting things done, because no one has ever accomplished big things by starting with the attitude, "We could give it a try, but it's probably not going to happen."

✳ Seeing Success

I wanted to really understand how a person has to think in order to win in any competitive arena, so after touring restaurants in Williamsburg, Virginia, I stopped in to see Bob Rotella at his house. Bob, one of the world's leading sports psychologists and an expert on peak performance, really drove this point home: "If you think of yourself as able to do something, you probably will do it. If you think of yourself as incapable, you probably won't." But believing that you can succeed is not the same thing as knowing exactly how you're going to get there. It means having faith that you and your people will find a way. If you don't already have the knowledge, you can find it. If you don't already have the resources, you can get them. It means believing that you and your team have the capacity to figure things out. And if you don't believe that, you need to spend some time thinking about why you don't. By fully examining why not, you'll identify barriers to your goal.

Are You Focused on the Positive? Yum! Brands sponsors a young golfer named J. B. Holmes, and in 2009 I was fortunate enough to be able to watch him play in my hometown of Louisville, Kentucky, as part of the U.S. Ryder Cup team. It was a tough match against the Europeans, and late in the day, Holmes was faced with a pivotal sixty-eight-yard shot over a trap. To my eyes, it looked practically impossible to get the ball anywhere near the pin.

I watched Holmes closely as he took what seemed like forever to consider his position. He opened and closed his eyes over and over again, almost as though he was in a trance, until he finally took his swing and hit the ball so it landed right next to the pin. He then made his birdie putt, which won him the pivotal match. Afterward, I asked him what he'd been thinking prior to taking the shot, and he replied, "I blocked out everything around me and thought about every good wedge shot I'd ever made. After that, I knew I was ready to hit it."

By contrast, early the next year, after playing a fantastic round on the final day of the Houston Open to qualify for a sudden-death play-off against Paul Casey, Holmes began the playoff on the eighteenth hole where three times he approached the ball to hit it and three times he backed away looking uncertain. When he finally hit the ball, he hooked it into the lake. Again, after the tournament I got a chance to ask Holmes what he'd been thinking, but this time he had a very different answer: "The wind was howling and I knew I had to be careful not to hit the water." Think water and water is probably what you'll get.

Do You Need to Change Your Perspective? Bob Rotella also told me about Paul Azinger, who happened to be leaving his house as I arrived. If you follow golf, you might recall that Azinger was having one of the best seasons of his golfing career when he was diagnosed with lymphoma, but that didn't get in his way for long. After an eight-month battle with the disease, he made a triumphant return to the game.

That in itself makes for a pretty good story. But it doesn't end there. After Azinger returned to golf, he grew frustrated by how he was playing, enough so that he turned to Rotella for help.

Rotella told me that he asked Azinger to bring over some tapes of him playing before he got sick. As they sat together and watched Azinger win tournament after tournament, Rotella turned to him and asked, "What were you thinking when you made all those shots?"

"Gosh, Bob," Azinger said, "I was thinking that I was the best player in the world and I was going to kick everyone's butt."

"And what do you think when you play now?"

"I've been thinking that after the cancer, I'm just happy to be alive, happy that I get a chance to play again." And that was the problem. He wasn't thinking like someone who could win. Rotella persuaded him to move past feeling lucky and refocus on thinking, practicing, and playing the way he had when he was at the top of his game. The story went on to have a very happy ending: Azinger left Bob's house and went straight to the Canadian Open, where he came in second. Then he won his first tournament since his illness in Hawaii a couple of months later. Instead of just being happy to be back on the tour, Rotella got Azinger to think and play like a winner again. The two go hand in hand.

Are you trying not to lose or are you trying to win? There is a difference. Rotella says it has been proven time and time again that when you see yourself a certain way, your behavior changes to suit that image of yourself.

* Prepare Your Mind to Win

Business and, for that matter, life are no different from golf in this way. You have to expect to win. In order to succeed, you have to be able to picture where you want to be and believe you can get there.

But how do you cultivate that belief? It's not an easy thing to do, but it is essential. The following are some ways that might help you adopt a more winning attitude:

Consider the Alternatives: If you are having a hard time picturing yourself succeeding, picture yourself failing instead, and see how that feels. Bonnie Hill, who, among many other accomplishments, was the director of the U.S. Office of Consumer Affairs under the first President Bush, thought very carefully about the consequences of not succeeding when, at the age of thirty, with a young child to support, her husband had a major heart attack.

At the time, she was working in a clerical position at Mills College in California and had no formal higher education. "It occurred to me that if I would end up being the breadwinner that I would really need to have a better way to make a living for my daughter," she said, "because my flashback took me back to the times when my mother and I were on welfare, and the last thing you want is to repeat that."

Hill didn't know how, exactly, she was going to get to a place of financial security for her family, but she did know she didn't have much of a choice. So she took the first step by going to the dean of admissions at Mills and asking if she could become a student. Even though she had yet to take the SATs and her high school grades weren't that hot, she did what she needed to do to get accepted into the college. But then it became a matter of how to pay for it. "I went to the president and I said, 'Look, I want to become a student. I can't afford tuition, so it would really be great if you'd waive it.' He'd never been approached by anyone like that before so he said yes before he knew what had happened."

But Hill didn't stop there. Everyone around her assumed that attending college while keeping her full-time job meant it would take her ten years to complete her education. But she found a quicker route. She took additional classes at two local community colleges in the evenings, four nights a week, and got the credits transferred to Mills, all the while caring for her young child and recovering husband. "I had to find a way to make a living that would support my family and I couldn't do it without an education," she explained. And in two-and-a-half years, she had her BA.

Hill's path to a college degree was so unusual that no one could have plotted it out beforehand. Instead she adopted the attitude of "I'll find a

If you don't have the intention to succeed, it's better to go do something else. It's a drive that you have inside, and I happen to have an incredible example of that, first with my father and then with my mother. Because when my father came to America, at fifteen years old, by boat, with not more than $10 in his pocket, if he didn't have intentionality to succeed, I don't think we would be here. And when he passed away in 1960, my mother was thirty-eight with six children. She had never worked and was very young. She just sat at that desk and started working and was able to maintain a family and also keep a business. I just hope I can emulate one tenth of the intentionality that they had.

—MASSIMO FERRAGAMO,
CHAIRMAN, FERRAGAMO USA

way." She didn't have (or didn't allow herself) the option of failing, and that, ultimately, is what allowed her to succeed. She went on to get a doctorate in education and now serves on our board of directors and is also the lead director for Home Depot.

There are always consequences to failure, whether it's missing out on a promotion, losing the respect of your colleagues, or even losing your job. A little bit of fear can be healthy, as long as you use it to open your eyes to the other side: That's what happens if you lose, but just imagine what it will be like if you win.

Search Out Inspiration: I once had the privilege of meeting and listening to mountain climber Erik Weihenmayer talk about his accomplishments at our Yum! Restaurants International convention in Prague. Weihenmayer has climbed the seven highest peaks on the seven continents of the world, which is a pretty big deal in and of itself, but something else that you should know about Erik is that he's blind.

As I listened to Erik describe his harrowing trip up to the 29,000-foot-high summit of Mount Everest—an accomplishment that nearly 90 percent of Everest climbers fail to realize—amid snowstorms, high winds, multi-thousand-foot drops, and worse, it occurred to me what an incredible example he was of taking people with him. Erik is a skilled climber in his own right, there's no doubt about that, but he also had to rely on his fellow climbers in some unique ways. The guy in front of him on the mountain wore a bell on his pack so Erik could hear where he was going. His fellow team members regularly called out warnings—"Death fall two feet to your right!" and things like that—to keep him out of harm's way.

Before Erik could even begin to put teams together to climb mountains, he had to get over a pretty big hurdle: He had to believe it could be done. Erik wasn't born blind; blindness happened to him gradually beginning at the age of thirteen, and, when it started, he said, "I wasn't thinking about a vision, I was thinking about survival, just getting through the day. Blindness was like a storm that had descended upon me with such force, such viciousness, I thought I'd be crushed by it. I remember sitting in the cafeteria and listening to all the food fights, all the jokes passing me by that I wanted to be a part of. And I wasn't afraid to go blind. What I was afraid of was that I'd be swept to the sidelines, that I'd be forgotten, that my life would be meaningless."

What changed things for Erik was a bit of inspiration he found in a pretty unlikely place, on a television show called *That's Incredible,* which aired in the 1980s. At first, Erik could still see a little out of one eye, and if he got really close to the set, he could watch TV. That's what he was doing one night when a segment came on featuring Terry Fox, a Canadian man who had lost a leg to cancer. As Erik remembers it: "Now most people in that situation would have just dug in and focused on survival. Terry did the exact opposite. He was still in the hospital when he decided he was going to run across Canada, east to west.

Our area is full of wars and problems and conflicts unlimited. And if you tell someone in a very stable market like the U.S. or like Japan, come to operate in the Middle East, they tell you, "Why? It's quite risky!" But we see this risk as an opportunity. That's why we invest in the Middle East and we'll keep investing in the Middle East today and tomorrow.

—MOATAZ AL-ALFI, CEO OF KUWAIT FOOD CO.

They fitted him with this old-style prosthetic leg. I remember him limping mile after mile, the miles taking a terrible toll on his body, and the look on Terry's face, it was an absolute contradiction. It was full of exhaustion yet, at the same time, full of exaltation." The desire to succeed was written all over his face.

What's interesting about inspiration is that it can snowball. Terry inspired Erik, who in turn went on to do some amazing things, and as he talked about them, Erik inspired me. Whenever I find myself in a negative frame of mind, thinking I can't do something, I just look around. You can find inspiring stories of people succeeding all over the place. And if they can do it, why can't you?

* Be Intentional About Belief

Your circumstances are probably not as dire as Bonnie Hill's after her husband got sick, or Erik Weihenmayer's when he lost his vision, but we can all recognize the power of their will to succeed. If you really care about something and want to see it happen, you have to be determined too. And you're going to have to communicate to others your determination by letting them know that you have taken a stake in the success of your Big Goal. My friend Bob Walter, the former chairman and CEO of Cardinal Health, once told me a story about the conquistador Hernán Cortés. It's said that when Cortés landed in South America with the intention of conquering the area, he burned their boats so there was no way for him or his people to go back. Now that's a guy who was intent on accomplishing his mission!

You have to ask yourself: What can I do to show people my will to succeed? What can I do to inspire in them the same belief that it can be done?

Nobody follows Eeyores. Remember the donkey from Winnie the Pooh who always thought it was going to rain? Imagine him trying to get people on his side and believing they could climb a mountain.

People want to follow leaders who believe they are capable of doing great things and who ignite that same belief in others. To be that type of leader, you have to choose a "can-do" mind-set.

mind-set check

"I can try"
versus
"We can do this!"

* Communicate Your Belief . . . and Sing It Loud

Kedibone Malatji is a KFC franchise owner in South Africa. She is a small business owner doing very normal, everyday business-owner type things, trying to keep her business growing and her employees engaged. And yet Malatji has the ability to cast the most amazing shadow of positive energy over every single member of her forty-five-person team.

Singing is a big part of the culture in South Africa, so a number of restaurants in our system there have songs they've made up to celebrate the company's principles of good customer service. It's a pretty amazing thing, but what's even more amazing is what I witnessed when I went to visit Malatji's restaurant: She and her team finished their song with a cheer. The team chanted to Malatji, "We believe in you!" who then chanted back, "I believe in you!" I saw this myself,

It's easy to be confident at seventy-four because life is what it is and life has been good, but the important thing is to have faith in yourself and have faith in what you're trying to accomplish. And I think if you do that and you get a little bit of success under your belt, all of a sudden one day it's like the little engine: I can do it, I can do it, I can do it. I'm a firm believer that I was inspired by a lot of people who taught me to believe that I was capable of so much more than I thought I could do myself.

—KEN LANGONE, COFOUNDER OF HOME DEPOT

so believe me when I tell you they didn't do this just because the boss told them to. I could feel their passion as they continued to chant back and forth like this until tears were literally running down cheeks.

I have never seen a more obvious example of the power of belief. We all want someone to believe in us; we all want to believe we have an opportunity to make our own corner of the world a little bit bigger, a little bit better. And if you don't think belief is important, consider this: Malatji's team has won just about every company award possible and her business has been so successful, that they are on track to open five new restaurants this year alone.

✳ Know Why You Believe

If your goal comes out of nowhere, you'll have a hard time believing in it. This notion takes into account everything we've talked about in this section so far about the leadership mind-set. You have to have a realistic picture of who you are and what you're capable of (chapter 2), you have to have a good sense of the knowledge you'll need to accomplish your goal (chapter 3), and you have to have faith in the people who will help you accomplish it (chapter 4). If you've worked through all those things, then you should be in a good position to believe it can be done. And in the next section, we'll talk about how to start turning that goal into a reality.

✳ Insights and Actions

Self-reflection

Assess yourself on the following items related to chapter 5, "You Have to Believe It Can Be Done":	Personal Opportunity	Personal Strength
1. I convey self-confidence and self-assurance when interacting with others.		
2. When faced with a challenge, I adopt a can-do attitude and a problem-solving perspective.		

Assess yourself on the following items related to chapter 5, "You Have to Believe It Can Be Done":	Personal Opportunity	Personal Strength
3. I view setbacks as an opportunity to learn, knowing they will help my success in the future.		
4. I choose a powerful mind-set when plans are derailed, then focus on getting back on track.		
5. I keep my personal and organiza-tional values in balance even when there are setbacks.		
6. I clearly demonstrate that I believe in every person on my team.		

Exercise

As you think about your Big Goal, what are five beliefs that give you the intentionality to achieve it? For example, a marketing manager who wanted to come up with a bold new campaign that would increase market penetration came up with these beliefs: (1) My people have creative minds; (2) They want to do good work; (3) They are capable of big ideas; (4) Customers will respond if we communicate with them in the right way; and (5) We are offering a superior product.

1.

2.

3.

4.

5.

* Learning Download for Part I: The Leadership Mind-set

• *Being yourself* is the best way to exhibit the kind of integrity a leader needs to get people to follow.

• *Being an avid learner* means that you prioritize knowledge and ideas over ego. Doing this will make you more open to hearing and respecting the ideas of others, which will make people more willing to come to you with good ideas.

• *You unleash the power of people* by believing in them, in their good intentions, and in their capacities to succeed. If you don't start with this belief, people won't follow you very far.

• *You have to believe* in your own capacity to get big things done. No one ever accomplished very much by starting off with the attitude, "Well, maybe it will work out."

• The lessons of all chapters in this section don't apply only to you. As a leader, you want to encourage those you lead to adopt more powerful mind-sets as well. *All* members of your team should be striving to be their best selves, to become avid learners, to build the potential of those around them, and to believe in the potential of the entire team to accomplish big things. That's the best way for all of you to reach your goals.

The preceding summary is intended to remind you how the lessons of this section will help you take people with you. To further reflect on these lessons and put them to work for you, go back through your answers to the Exercises and Self-reflection questions at the end of each chapter. Next, answer the following questions, which will help you determine where you need to focus your efforts the most as you build your skills as a leader.

• What are the biggest aha's you picked up about yourself while reading the chapters in "Get Your Mind-set Right"?

- Of those aha's, what are the two or three that, if you worked on them, would have the greatest impact on your Big Goal?

- What will you start doing differently tomorrow as a result of what you've learned in this section?

No one said that Taking People with You was going to be simple. The stories that follow are from people who have been through my leadership program and have had their own difficulties in maximizing their potential in a particular area. Everyone has a unique set of strengths and weaknesses. The more you understand what yours are, the better chance you have of building on your strengths and compensating for your weaknesses. I hope you'll take some inspiration from how Robert and Joanna did something about those things that were difficult for them to overcome.

Robert on "Being Your Best Self"

I consider myself an introvert, so being myself in a group situation has always been hard for me. But after listening to feedback about my leadership skills from people both above and below me, I started to hear a common criticism: People wished I was more open with them, that I was more forthcoming about what I was thinking and what I was feeling about things. Before hearing that, I thought that talking about my feelings in a business situation was not very relevant at best, and self-indulgent at worst. But when it came time to assess my own skills in this area, I couldn't ignore what I'd been hearing.

I had to force myself, even to the point of discomfort, to become more open and let people in more. But I've realized how important it actually is for an organization to connect with its leadership, and it's very hard for them to do that unless they understand the values that actually drive that leader.

Joanna on "Unleashing the Power of People"

As a team leader, I was supposed to do these one-on-one sessions with each member of my team as a status report/performance review. I realized that after I scheduled these sessions, things were coming up that were pulling me in different directions. So I kept canceling the sessions to deal with whatever was at hand. The problem was, I had always told my people that they were my number-one priority. But how could they believe that if I kept canceling or pushing back their one-on-ones? I really had to look closely at what I was doing, acknowledge the message I was sending, even when I didn't mean to, and work on adjusting my actions to match the priorities I had set forth. I had to figure out how to change and not let everyday stresses get in the way of being the kind of leader I wanted to be.

part two

have a plan

strategy, structure, culture

i n this section, we will switch from thinking to doing. I trust you're now armed with the right mind-set to accomplish Big Goals, but what do you do to make them happen? Obviously, you'll need a plan to take people with you.

My friend Larry Senn once shared with me a simple Senn Delaney model for developing a plan, which I've used over and over again. It has three basic parts, which, though they reinforce one another, need to be considered in the order in which they are presented:

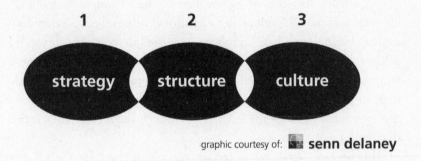

graphic courtesy of: **senn delaney**

1. Strategy: With your team, you need to clearly identify where you're going and what you want to get done.

2. Structure: You need to reinforce your strategy by putting the right resources and processes in place so your people can help you execute your plan.

3. Culture: You have to create an environment that reinforces the strategy and structure by engaging your people and encouraging the behaviors you want.

This is not a book on how to develop a business strategy, but there are numerous books that can help you determine what actions you need to take to meet your specific business goals. Instead, this section will cover how to take people with you through each aspect of your plan.

The first three chapters in this section have to do with the first part—the Strategy—and in these I'll talk about how to make sure you have one that your people can rally around. Chapter 9 covers the second part, the Structure your people need to support your strategy. Finally, chapter 10 deals with the Culture aspect of your plan.

At Yum! we have used this model for every type of change effort, big or small, since our spin-off from PepsiCo. It's a deceptively simple formula, however. You must never forget how interconnected these pieces are. Miss a step or do them in the wrong order, and you won't have a complete plan. As Matt Killen, the twenty-six-year-old wunderkind golf coach for the likes of Kenny Perry, Chad Campbell, and J. B. Holmes, told me: "It's not good to Band-Aid things, because they continue to bleed. If you have a problem, you need to fix it right. If you try to shortcut it, it looks like a shortcut." Remember, there is always a temptation, especially when you see improvement in results, to skip steps in your plan. Don't get ahead of yourself. If your plan is a good one, one that's right for the long term, work through every step. If you skip, you'll pay.

This became very clear to me when I was at the Pepsi-Cola Company during a time when the business was in need of transformation. Historically, Pepsi had made its money by selling concentrate, the base components for Pepsi, Mountain Dew, and its other brands. The company sold concentrate to independent franchisees, who would invest in plants and warehouses, manufacture the products, and then make money by selling the finished brands to customers, the businesses that stocked Pepsi products in the grocery stores and convenience stores of the world. But in the late 1980s, that began to change. Major national accounts like Walmart and Costco were becoming more and more powerful, and they wanted to deal with one point of contact versus countless local franchise bottlers. Given the size and growing importance of this emerging customer base, PepsiCo made the decision to consolidate its bottling network. Pepsi started to buy up a number of bottling operations until we owned about 65 percent of the system. For the first time, we had to figure out how to bottle our products and deal with customers ourselves on a very broad scale. It quickly became very apparent that we just weren't very good at all this. We had invested a ton of money but were getting returns that were clearly not up to snuff.

Pepsi president Craig Weatherup rightly realized that this meant a sea change in the organization. Pepsi was going to have to learn to become more customer focused and make money at the same time. With the help of consultants, we came up with this notion of becoming a Right Side Up company, a concept that was illustrated using an inverted pyramid. The idea was that the front line was now at the top of that pyramid because they were the ones who had contact with the customers. Management was at the bottom of the pyramid because they were there to serve and support those on the front line.

Weatherup is an incredibly smart guy and he was passionately behind this. We had meetings all around the country at bottling plants where we presented this new concept: the Right Side Up culture that would define PepsiCo going forward. The problem wasn't that it was a bad concept; it was simply an incomplete one. The bottlers were all for it, but they had practical concerns: We want to put the customers first and make them happy, too, but what does that mean? What do customers want from us exactly? And how do we give it to them?

The bottlers were right. In our efforts to redefine the company, management had skipped over two crucial steps, Strategy and Structure, and concentrated primarily on Culture. Because of that, we had to go home and start over from the beginning.

We didn't throw out the idea of a Right Side Up company. Instead, we got more definition about what that meant. We moved from a carbonated soft drink company to a "total beverage company" (Strategy), which meant offering more product variety to our customers, such as bottled water and iced teas, in addition to soft drinks. Doing this, however, required that we revamp some of our processes so that, for example, our delivery trucks carried more than just our carbonated soft drinks, adding products like Aquafina, Lipton teas, and Ocean Spray juices (Structure). It was only after we got the strategy and structure right that the customer-focused culture really came to life. The result was substantially better performance.

I'm confident that following the Strategy, Structure, Culture model, in the right order, will pay off for you, as well, as you pursue your Big Goal.

6 * strategy: tell it like it is . . . and how it could be

my mentor, Andy Pearson, was a master at establishing truth in his business. When he was chairman of our company, there was something he used to say over and over again, like a motto: "See the world the way it really is, not how you wish it to be."

Andy was one of the most tough-minded leaders I've ever known. He had a knack for getting quickly to the heart of any issue, and he never minced words. I remember one of the first business meetings we had at Yum. A senior executive presented this chart with a big arrow pointing upward, showing that our return on invested capital had risen from 3 percent to 5 percent. The reality was, the bar graph on the chart looked a lot more impressive than the actual results, which were, in fact, way below our cost of capital. Andy, who clearly wasn't born yesterday, just looked at him and said in that straightforward way of his, "Listen pal, I want you to know that this is the last time in this company that we will ever celebrate mediocrity."

To start working toward any goal, first you need to define reality for yourself and for your team. Too many people have a tendency to sugarcoat things, but that doesn't help improve performance. Andy may have prided himself on his toughness (*Fortune* magazine once named him one of the "top 10 toughest bosses in the world," a designation that he felt honored by, even framing the magazine's cover and hanging it in his office), but he didn't say what he said just to be negative. He said it to give framework to the facts—a 2 percent jump is certainly better than a loss, but it was more like doing a curb chin-up rather than a real one. It wasn't exactly the kind of accomplishment that any of us should be writing home about.

> *I think defining reality is relatively easy in situations where you've got issues and problems, because I think most of the time those problems are evident to the organization. Actually, it's liberating for the organization for the leader to define it, because often people think that those subjects are taboo, that we can't talk about those kinds of things. What's harder is where a business is doing well. It's very easy in an environment like that for people to get complacent. What's just as important, though, is to define reality in that situation, because all sorts of studies have shown that the most successful companies are those companies that reinvent themselves even when they're doing well.*
>
> —GRAHAM ALLAN, CHIEF EXECUTIVE OFFICER, YUM! RESTAURANTS INTERNATIONAL

This is a crucial role of any leader. In business, we tend to be inundated with lots of facts and figures, but what do they really mean? It's the leader's job to create the context and present the story of that data. Are we doing 2 percent better than last year? Yes. But does that mean we're doing well? Are we beating our competition? Can we be doing better? What should we be aiming for? Telling it like it is means more than just presenting the facts; it means showing what they mean—and what they could mean in the future—for your business or for any task you're working on.

* Reality *Plus*

Your strategy starts by getting everyone on the same page, but you can't stop there. You can't just tell people how bad things are and then leave them be. You can't even tell them how good things are and then leave them be. You must define reality while also showing people where that reality can take them. Defining reality and creating hope go hand in hand here. As Napoléon Bonaparte once said, "A leader is a dealer in hope." Or put another way by a less controversial figure, the late author and philosopher Sydney Banks said, "Never forget that hope is a very important ally that leads to miraculous things."

Creating hope means showing people where the facts in front of them could lead. If things are bad, people need to understand that, but they also need to know that things can get better. And if things are good, people need to understand that, too, and be congratulated for their part in the success. And then they need to be reminded that there will be a lot of work ahead to keep things going in the right direction.

Where necessary, you may also have to give people reason to move toward the hopeful reality you've shown them by establishing urgency or "creating a burning platform." People don't really change until there is enough pain to force them to change, but you better believe that if they're standing on a platform that's on fire, they will be seriously motivated to jump. When your business is in a really bad place, you've already got a burning platform. But if you're doing OK, you will have to create a totally different reason to motivate people to raise the bar.

✳ What Is "Reality"?

In chapter 2 of this book, I asked you to take a hard look at yourself: what your values are, what your strengths and weaknesses are, how people perceive you, and how you perceive yourself. Now it's time to do the same thing with your business. Take that same analytical eye and turn it on your business with brutal honesty.

But what does "reality" mean exactly? One of the best ways to approach this is to dig for insights in four key areas:

1. **Customer Reality:** Nothing should motivate you more than what your customer is telling you. You can find out what your customers are thinking by using formal methods, like customer satisfaction surveys, focus groups, or problem detection studies. But you should also use some informal methods. Talk to customers directly as often as you can. Make an effort to see what they

Right now, we have a terrifically big barrier at Pizza Hut because this bad economy has put a spotlight on the fact that we are premium priced; people can't afford us. That's pretty easy to explain. I stood up at our fall business conference and told all of our key operators and franchisees, "I know you all have opinions about why our sales might not be what they should be. Listen to the customers. The customers are telling you in very plain language we're too expensive. Now we have to go out and do something about it." The outside-in perspective of customers saying "you are too expensive" really hit home with those guys. They went home, and they actually did something about their pricing, and now we have the best value perception in our category.

—SCOTT BERGREN, CHIEF EXECUTIVE OFFICER, PIZZA HUT

see. If you're in a retail business, make unannounced visits to your stores so you can see the place the way your customers do; if you're in a manufacturing business, take home and use your own products; if you work as a manager in a call center, spend some time answering the phones; and so on.

One of the best tactics I've used for helping my team understand the customer is to create a shared experience by going out as a group and paying visits to our restaurants. I've even arranged bus tours with customers and team members together, where we visit locations and then share our thoughts about what we experienced. It's a great way to bring team members together and get them on the same page about what's happening in your business.

2. **Team Reality:** Ask questions of your team members: What's working? What's not working? What would you do if you were me? Someone once told me the most powerful way to motivate people is to listen to them. I couldn't agree more. In fact, I think "What do you think?" is the most powerful question you can use to engage people.

You have to remember when you ask people questions like this, however, that your position as leader can make you intimidating. It's important to be as approachable as possible so that people feel comfortable telling you the truth. Approach people as equals, like you're one of them, because you are. One of the best pieces of advice I've ever gotten came from Jack Byrum, the Dallas image consultant I worked with early in my career: "Don't look up, don't look down. Always look straight ahead when dealing with people."

Another method for getting to the truth of your team reality is to encourage healthy debate. Business author and former vice chairman of GE and CEO of Allied Signal Larry Bossidy talks about the importance of valuing "truth over harmony," meaning that it's more important to encourage an atmosphere where everyone puts their cards on the table than one where everyone agrees.

3. **Competitive Reality:** Know your enemy and see how you stack up in comparison. You have to keep the performance of your competitors front and center in your mind. In my business, for example, after our

> *One of the first things I did is, I asked the leaders, How do you think you're performing versus the competition? The first thing you want leaders to do is recognize the truth, the whole truth, and nothing but the truth. A lot of them make excuses, but literally, and I'm really not kidding, our margins were half of our competition's. I wanted people to acknowledge that our performance was terrible. And then, when you dug deeper, it was terrible by branch, it was terrible in expenses, it was terrible by product. It was terrible on all these different levels. To me, the first thing was just acknowledging that.*
>
> —JAMIE DIMON, CHAIRMAN AND CEO, JPMORGAN CHASE, DEFINING REALITY WHEN HE FIRST JOINED THE COMPANY AFTER BEING HEAD OF BANK ONE

first ten years, we had quadrupled our stock price. That's a real accomplishment, but it wasn't the whole story. We were doing a great job of expanding our business and adding new stores, but as I mentioned earlier, McDonald's was doing an even better job of growing sales from its existing restaurants. We clearly still had work to do, and that one fact gave us both a goal (to outperform McDonald's) and a focus (to increase sales from our established restaurants).

4. **Financial Reality**: This one is pretty obvious, but you have to know your numbers and compare them to past performance as well as to what's possible for the future. There's nothing more sobering than the cold hard facts of where you stand, with your peers and against your competitors. That's why every successful business I know racks and stacks from top to bottom the financial results of its people and business units. The best performance shows what's possible; the worst performance puts the right kind of pressure on the pride and survival instincts required to improve. Every business, every enterprise, every project needs a financial scorecard if money is anywhere in the equation—and it usually is.

* Reality Work Sheet

Use the explanations on the preceding pages as examples and then define the reality of your situation as it applies to your Big Goal. What is your reality in each of these four key areas?

1. Customer Reality

2. Team Reality

3. Competitive Reality

4. Financial Reality

tool: hotshot replaces me

This is one of my favorite tools, because I love my job and I want to keep it! Imagine that tomorrow you are being replaced by someone who is a real hotshot. That person's goal is to do a much better job in your position than you did. He or she will start by pointing out all your shortcomings and missed opportunities. Then that person will tell everyone how he or she will do the job so much better than you.

Now take what that person would say, get a healthy dissatisfaction with your performance, and go for breakthrough results now!

To Use This Tool

To help push yourself to see your business and your performance for what it is, ask yourself these questions:

• What shortcomings and missed opportunities could a hotshot find if that person wanted to show how bad your performance was?

• What would a hotshot start doing to show how much better he is than you?

• What realities would a hotshot point to that you had been ignoring?

Now set a plan to do yourself what a hotshot would do. Attack the unfinished business!

© *John O'Keeffe, BusinessBeyondtheBox.com*

∗ Creating Hope

Part of what you're digging for when you gather data on your four kinds of reality is not just a picture of where your company is today; you're also looking for evidence that the goal you're trying to accomplish can be done or that the future you're picturing is possible. If, for example, your company is in a position where it needs a big turnaround fast, you want to find proof that silences those who don't believe it's possible. You never want your people to feel that they have to follow you in blind faith. Instead you want to ground them in as much substance as possible to show it can be done.

This proof can come in different forms. Laying out your game plan is crucial, to give people confidence in your methods (more on this in the coming chapters). You should present evidence that the strides you've made are working, and keep doing this as you make more along the way. Also look for examples of others who have had similar successes. When I was watching the Orange Bowl national championship football game in 2000, I was really impressed to see that Oklahoma coach Bob Stoops had crowded the sidelines with all-Americans from past Oklahoma championship teams. This gave his players hope and confidence that helped carry them to victory.

You simply have to have hope. If you find yours is waning, you need to look for ways to restore it for yourself and your team. Having hope wasn't always easy when Yum! Brands was first spun off from PepsiCo. PepsiCo was, and still is, a successful, well-respected company that we had all signed up to be part of. Then one day we woke up to find that they had decided to shed our brands because we'd been a drag on their earnings. That signaled to most people that PepsiCo leaders didn't have a lot of faith in the ability of our brands to make money. If they had, why would they have gotten rid of us? That's a dubious beginning for a new company.

John Weinberg, the late and truly great former chairman of Goldman Sachs, was on our board of directors at the time, and one day he came in and said he wanted to share something with me. He showed me a sheet of paper that spelled out the ten characteristics that Goldman Sachs had identified for high-quality companies. We looked at it together and realized that our new company lived up to every single characteristic on that page except for two things: We didn't have a track record of growth, obviously, because we were just starting out, and we didn't have a strong balance sheet because our spin-off from PepsiCo had come with a boatload of debt. But we knew that, with time, we could get those things right. That gave me hope, so I shared the sheet with everyone on my team to give them hope too, using data to show how we lived up to most of the characteristics. It helped us believe that we had a *realistic* opportunity to be a high-performing company in the future. And that was the kind of hope we needed.

goldman sachs's ten characteristics of a high-performing company

1. High-quality product or service and sustainable competitive advantage.

2. Superior management with a demonstrated desire to act in shareholders' interests.

3. Compound earnings growth rate of 10–12 percent over the last ten years.

4. Consistency/predictability/quality of reported earnings.

5. Projected growth in earning power of at least 10 percent over three years.

6. A strong balance sheet.

7. High profitability.

8. Generation of free cash flow.

9. International competitiveness.

10. Reasonable purchase price.

❋ Telling Isn't Selling

Telling someone to go do something is not the best way to get them to do it. People, I don't care who they are, like to discover their own solutions to problems. Think about how you feel: Don't you feel the biggest sense of ownership over ideas, actions, or conclusions you've come to on your own, as opposed to something you've been told you have to do? The fact is, "I said it, so do it" or "I did it, so you do it" just doesn't cut it for motivating and inspiring the people you need to take with you.

You have to believe that you will come up with the best solutions by involving others. That means that it's your job to define reality in an emotional way that creates a clear case for change and hope for the future, but then realize that people are best won over when they draw their own conclusions. Share all four categories of reality with your team and then ask them what they would do about it.

This takes confidence, and it's a real break from authoritarian leadership styles of the past, whereby the leader told you what to do and you went out and did it. That style doesn't work so well in today's business world. You can't just tell people to drink the water. It's best when they decide for themselves that they *want* to drink the water.

Earlier in this chapter, I included a quote from Scott Bergren, CEO of Pizza Hut, who used customer reality to convince the franchisees in his system that they needed to make some changes in their pricing. That was a pretty big shift in thinking for franchisees. But when customers were asked why they weren't satisfied with Pizza Hut, 51 percent cited price/value. They also listed numerous places where they believed they got better value for their money, including McDonald's and Subway, branded frozen pizzas found in grocery stories, and local pizza places. But Scott didn't tell his franchisees what to do about this problem. He presented the facts, made a compelling case for change, and then asked, What are we going to do about our pricing problem?

About 80 percent of Pizza Hut franchisees adjusted their pricing without anyone telling them what to do. One of those franchisees even came up with our most popular new promotion, $10 Pizza Any Way You Want It, which allows customers to get a large pizza with their choice of crust and as many toppings as they want (including our specialty options) for one low price.

> *No situation in business, when you really think about it, is hopeless. If you're breathing and you can get up in the morning, you've got a chance.*
>
> —DAVE DORMAN, CHAIRMAN OF MOTOROLA

* Constantly Identify the Unfinished Business

Part of defining reality for people is identifying the work your team still needs to do to get where you want to go. This is where you, as leader, help make sense of the reality of your current situation by framing it in terms of these questions: What's next? Where do we go from here? What's our unfinished business?

If you don't keep asking yourself and your team these questions, you could be headed for some big surprises. Motorola was among the world leaders when mobile telephones got started, with the highest selling mobile product in history, the Razr, but then pretty much blew it. Dave Dorman, who is now the chairman of Motorola, explained it to me this way: "They sold a couple hundred million of the Razr. That's probably about ten times as many iPods as have been sold. It was a $15 billion a year product . . . one product. That success created, I think, a lot of hubris. But it's a very short-cycle business. It changes literally almost like fashion. In a six-month period, they went from selling thirty million a quarter to two million a quarter, and there was not a new product behind it. So Motorola hit the wall." Sales of the Razr started to decline rapidly, and the company's revenues went from about $30 billion to $8 billion annually within a span of just eighteen months. Motorola lost its place at the top and would spend years trying to get back in the game.

tool: second set mentality

In tennis, the person who wins the first set will often lose the second, even if she won the first by a large margin. Why? Because the loser now knows her opponent's game and may become that much more motivated now that she's playing from behind. Or perhaps the winner becomes complacent about her performance now that she has a win under her belt. But in reality, the strategy and level of play that won her the first set no longer applies because the game has changed. In tennis, just as in business or in life, the game is always changing.

You've probably heard the famous quote "Insanity is doing the same thing over and over and expecting different results." But because the game is always changing, it also doesn't make sense to do the same thing over and over and expect the *same* results.

This tool is useful for defining your unfinished business and refocusing on your goals. What's coming next? What are the possibilities? If business has been good and you've been winning, then you'll need to play even harder from now on to make sure you keep it that way. And if things haven't been going so well, then declaring a "second set" is an opportunity to do better. At root here is the idea that we can always start over. No matter where we've been, we can enter a second set, where things will be different.

Second Set Tactics

This tool allows you to draw a line in the sand and demand new, different, extraordinary performance, even when you are doing very well.

Importantly, it still allows you to congratulate your people on the successes they had in the first set. This is unusually helpful, because "we must do better" techniques tend to focus more on how bad people are.

Start identifying what will be tougher in the second set. Once you do this, you can stop tolerating the nonperformers from the first set. Often when a company is winning the first set, no one pays serious attention to the parts of the company or the people who aren't performing as well as they should—you're winning, so there's no need to address them. But by declaring a second set, you establish a new situation, with new challenges, and that allows you to deal with the underperforming parts of your team or organization.

© John O'Keeffe, BusinessBeyondtheBox.com

* Insights and Actions

Self-reflection

Assess yourself on the following items related to chapter 6, "Tell It Like It Is":	Personal Opportunity	Personal Strength
1. I create the type of environment where people are not afraid to speak up or contradict my point of view.		
2. I have a systematic way of seeking the truth from my customers, my competitors, and my team.		
3. I regularly ask my team what we are doing right and what we are doing wrong in the business.		
4. I insist on rigorous discussion and productive conflict on critical priorities.		
5. When defining reality in tough situations, I always create hope for the future.		

Exercises

1. If some hotshot replaced you tomorrow, where would he or she say you missed the boat in telling it like it really is? Customers? Team? Financial? Competition?

2. What's keeping you from defining reality in that area?

7

* strategy: create a vision and personalize it

O nce you've defined reality for the people you lead, the next step is to develop a shared vision for where you want to go next. After a meeting with his team during which he had laid out an inspiring view of their future, a KFC franchisee from Tennessee, Charlie Middleton, said to me in his deep baritone, Deputy Dog–like voice, "A road to nowhere is hard to build." What he meant was that it's a lot easier to get somewhere if you know where you're headed. I couldn't agree more. When constructing a plan to achieve your goal, it's essential that you have a clear idea of the end point first, before you start drawing a road map for how to get there.

What do I mean by a vision? It's your idea of what the future will look like when you achieve your Big Goal, what the benefits are, what the outcome or results will be. If you can create a vision for what you want to get done and make it feel relevant to the people you lead, then you're going to be well on your way.

When creating a vision, think about your target audience, the people you have to take with you. You have to create a vision that the people you lead can look at and say:

1. I understand it.

2. I know that my customers, or the people we need to win over, will like it.

3. I can get excited about it.

4. I can make it happen.

For example, in 1998, after our spinoff from PepsiCo, I wanted to talk about my vision for where I saw us headed as a new company. When I thought about it (with the help and input of my team, of course), the success of our restaurant brands boiled down to one thing: making people happy. Good food makes people happy. If we can give them a great customer experience on top of that, they'll be even happier. If we give them value for their money, so they can keep a bit more in their pockets, well, that makes people happy too. So the vision we came up with was to "Put a YUM on people's faces around the world."

The vision I set forth satisfied each of the four points above, and all of us, from our restaurant workers to our lawyers, could get behind the idea. I handwrote a letter and sent it with this vision statement (or as I called it back then, our passion statement) to all our restaurant general managers and above-store leaders around the world to get their attention and give it a personal touch. (By the way, if you're wondering why the letterhead says Tricon, it's because that was our original name after the spinoff, one which I happily changed to the more memorable Yum! Brands when I became CEO.)

As John O'Keeffe, who created the Future Back tool that follows, said, "Make sure it's a concept of the future that drives what you do in the present."

David C. Novak
Vice Chairman and President

Tricon Global Restaurants, Inc.
PO Box 32220
Louisville, KY 40232-2220
Tel 502 456 8900

Dear Teammates,

Last week Andy and I teamed up with Tricon's senior leaders to review our 1998 annual operating plans. WOW... do we have a lot of great ideas in the works! The key now is to work together and make them happen. That's why we spent a day talking about how we're going to work together... the kind of leadership principles you and I should live by ... the kind of teamwork we know drives performance at our restaurants.

I've attached these principles for you to think about. (I look at them every day!)

As you know, words don't mean anything unless they are backed by action. The way all of us go about our work to PUT YUMS ON OUR CUSTOMERS FACES ☺ represents the key to our growth as people and as a business. If these principles are important enough to publish, they are important enough to live by. It's up to all of us to walk the talk. Let's do it!

YUM TO YOU,

David

tool: future back

Future ⇒ Present

Imagine a step-change possibility for the future first, then take massive action in the present to achieve it.

The idea here is to avoid falling into the habit of thinking and discussing the past first, then the present, and then the future. It's a myth that you have to get right about the past before you can take action in the present in the hope of creating a better future. Focusing first on the past can lead to endless, useless argument while you sort out "the hairball of right history."

Instead, use this tool to ensure that you start with a view of the future; then make sure your actions today are based on moving toward that future, rather than attempting to correct the past. When you find yourself or others talking about the past, change the conversation by saying, "Let's move from the past to the future."

Using This Tool When Establishing a Plan to Achieve Your Big Goal

• Visualize what the future will look like when you have achieved your goal.

• Then identify the actions you must take to reach that future vision.

• Decide what has to be accomplished each day/week to drive it to completion.

© *John O'Keeffe, BusinessBeyondtheBox.com*

* Create a Noble Cause

It's not just you who has to care about your vision for your business; it has to appeal to everyone involved in making it happen. In order to do all this, your vision has to inspire. Every employee, whether it's someone working a shift for minimum wage or a high-level executive, wants to be a part of something bigger. People don't want to go to work to just do their job. They are most motivated when they know that what they're doing counts and they are helping the team drive toward a powerful vision of the future. It's the leader's job to give them that vision in a way that ignites their hearts and minds.

Your job as a leader is to give people something they can get excited about. Making money is not enough to inspire anyone over the long term. After all, just about any business could set a goal like "beat last year's performance" or "grow profits by *x* percent." But does that really get anyone fired up? What's special about it?

A good vision invites people to be part of something bigger than themselves; it gives them a noble cause to participate in. The Starbucks vision statement, for example, isn't anything as obvious as "to make great coffee"; it's "to inspire and nurture the human spirit, one person, one cup, and one neighborhood at a time." The Walt Disney Company aspires, simply and profoundly, "to make people happy." Our own vision at Yum! Brands has evolved since that letter I wrote in 1998. Now it's to be "the defining global company that feeds the world." These are things that pretty much anyone can feel passionate about.

A lot of big companies, even the best of them, have stumbled in this area. Bill Weldon, CEO

I articulated this notion of "Performance with Purpose" for PepsiCo. Now performance is what PepsiCo is known for, that's what drives the company. But performance alone is not going to carry us into the future. I always say to our people, we operate with a license from society, which means we cannot add costs to society. We have to make sure that we help society. We are big enough to be a little country ourselves, so we have a duty. And the three things that we absolutely have to do are: One, we are committed to transforming our portfolio to have a balance of treats and healthy eats. Second, we want to be environmentally a very responsible entity, whether it's water usage, energy usage, or packaging waste. And third, we want to make sure every person who comes to PepsiCo not just has a living, but can make a life.

—INDRA NOOYI, CEO OF PEPSICO

of Johnson & Johnson, once told me that his company had a tagline that they put on just about everything: "The world's most diversified healthcare company." It may have been true and it may be pretty impressive, but Weldon said: "To me, that's not emotional. You need something emotive that people can relate to. So a few years ago, we sat down and we wrote what we call a caring statement, which basically says, 'We care for the world one person at a time.' And that resonates." They tested it with employees, customers, doctors, and healthcare providers, and it resonated with every group.

Google: To organize the world's information and make it universally accessible and useful.

Walmart: To give ordinary folks the chance to buy the same things as rich people.

The Walt Disney Company: To make people happy.

Starbucks: To inspire and nurture the human spirit, one person, one cup, and one neighborhood at a time.

P&G: We will provide branded products and services of superior quality and value that improve the lives of the world's customers, now and for generations to come.

Yum! Brands: To be the defining global company that feeds the world.

✳ Power Language

Words on a page are just that. You need to be careful that the words you choose to explain your goal and communicate your vision capture the attention of your target audience and inspire them to act.

One night I was watching a *60 Minutes* segment featuring Jack

Welch. He was talking about the need to get an organization pumped up about what really mattered. He believed quality was critical to his company, GE, but he didn't just say to his people, "Quality is important." He said he literally "went nuts" about quality, communicating its importance in everything the company did, from advertising to determining bonuses.

This got me thinking about one goal that was set early in our company, which was to improve customer satisfaction. Everyone can understand something like that, but I didn't think we'd made enough progress at getting our people to listen and respond to the voice of the customer. So that very night I decided to change the way we talked about it to give it more emphasis. "Customer focus" became "customer mania," and I started talking about the need to *go crazy* over understanding the needs of our customers and making them happy.

I quickly found that customer mania got everyone's attention. It elicited a reaction. It didn't sound like every other company out there that talks about the need to be focused on customers. It seriously and dramatically elevated the importance of the idea behind it. And now we have a much more customer-focused organization, one that measures its people on their ability to be customer maniacs.

To give another example, when Randall Stephenson became CEO of AT&T in 2007, he wanted to cause a shift in thinking within the organization. The company had always been grounded in their wireline business, but that was the past and he wanted people to be looking toward the future. And the future was wireless, because "that's where the growth was," he told me. So he summed up the new strategy in just two very memorable, very powerful words: "Mobilize everything." It was impossible not to get the message from that.

As the leader, you need to think carefully about the words you choose. Use the tool that follows to help you think through how best to impart your vision. Remember, it's not just the content of what you say, it's also how you say it that matters.

tool: emotional word picture

Emotional Word Pictures are formed when you use powerful language to put your goal into words, just as in the quote below.

A step-change goal works best when the words you use to describe it reach out and grab people's attention, capturing their hearts as well as their minds. The words should put an image in people's minds and a fire in their bellies.

In one of his State of the Union addresses, President Obama talked about how he believed the United States needed to elevate the importance of education in our culture. By way of example, he cited South Korea, where they believe educators are so important, they use very different language to describe their roles. They don't call them teachers, they call them "nation builders."

When creating an emotional word picture for your Big Goal, use the dinner party test to determine whether you've come up with an effective one. Ask yourself: How would I describe my goal to someone I just met at a dinner party in a way that might get that person emotionally interested?

More Examples

"Opening the highways to all mankind." —Ford Motor Co., 1925

"To change the image around the world of Japanese products as poor in quality." —Sony, 1950

"To achieve one person, one computer" —Apple, 1970s

"To be the most successful restaurant business, not just in China, but in the world." —Yum! China

© John O'Keeffe, BusinessBeyondtheBox.com

Avoid the tranquilizing drug of gradualism.
—MARTIN LUTHER KING JR.

* Personalize the Vision

I want to emphasize that you don't have to be a CEO to put these principles and tools into action. These concepts don't apply just to grand vision statements for large companies. They work on every level. When considering the goal you want to meet or the initiative you're tying to accomplish, ask yourself, What effect will making this happen have on people?

Everything comes back to people. Saving money improves quality of life. Improving customer service scores makes for a more enjoyable day for those who experience good service . . . maybe even causing them to pass on those good feelings to someone else. If an administrative assistant can significantly cut down on the use of paper, that can bring down the cost of doing business, which can keep the cost of products low for the consumer (not to mention the positive impact on the environment).

In our company, we ask: What are you doing in your piece of Yum! to help make us the defining global company that feeds the world? People answer with their own visions, depending on what they do. Brian Goldstein, one of our leading Taco Bell operators, has a vision for each of his restaurants "to be the best quick-service restaurant on the block." And Jonathan Blum, our chief public affairs officer, came up with a vision statement for our World Hunger Relief effort that dovetails perfectly with that of the organization, which is "to give every employee, company and franchisee the opportunity to help leave the world better than we found it by truly making an impact on this global crisis." Now that's a noble cause that everyone can relate to.

You need people to take your vision and make it their own in order to cascade the message. After all, you can't expect to always be around to repeat it. Noel Tichy, a professor at the University of Michigan business school, called this having a "teachable point of view." As a leader, you need to describe your goal in clear, simple, and impactful terms to your team members so that they can make that vision relevant to their own functions and teach it to their own people. The most successful messages are communicated this way, and that's one of the reasons why we've had Tichy participate in our Leadership Development Council at Yum! and emphasized his idea of leaders as teachers up and down our organization. We even use the word *coach* in place of *boss* to reinforce the concept. I often challenge people to come up with an elevator speech for their "teachable point of view," because if you can't communicate why your goal is important in quick and convincing terms in the time it takes for an elevator ride, then how can you expect anyone else to be able to carry your message?

Setting forth a bold and convincing vision actually inspires people to make it their own. You may not be in a position where you can set a vision as big or as broad as the examples I cited from Google or Starbucks, but you can still set a vision for your Big Goal much as Brian Goldstein did. He thought about what would appeal to his target audience—the employees in his restaurant—and he gave them something to shoot for that they could be proud to achieve.

tool: from-to

Now, I realize most people don't run companies, but everyone has initiatives they need to get people excited about executing. To this end, one of the tools I've always used while coming up through the ranks is what I call from-to. One way to frame your vision is to talk about how you are going to go "from" the current status quo "to" a much more powerful future.

John O'Keeffe describes essentially the same idea, in our Achieving Breakthrough Results program, as going from System A to System B. System A encompasses those things that allow you just to get by in your work. They are the everyday things you think or do that lead to acceptable, ordinary results. Perhaps they lead to some incremental changes (if you recall the tool I presented in chapter 1, Picture Step-Change, these are the kind of changes that take you from 3.5 percent to 4 percent sales growth over the course of a year) but not the kind of things that truly excite people.

System B, in contrast, encompasses those things that are a step-change away from how you've done business in the past. These are the powerful, extraordinary ways of thinking or acting that lead to big results. I truly believe that everyone wants a chance to be extraordinary, and presenting people with a more extraordinary vision for how things can be is the first step toward getting there.

Here are some examples of how we used this tool in our organization to change people's thinking around the importance of building know-how. To elaborate on the first example in the list, we discovered that only people in certain positions considered the idea of innovation to be an important part of their job. But we wanted everyone to be thinking about new and better ways of doing business, no matter what the job title. If an executive assistant could learn a new software program that made her workday more efficient, then that was her being innovative.

From System A to System B: Building Know-how

Innovation is not my job.	Innovation is everyone's job.
I'm drowning in information.	Building know-how helps me separate the significant from the irrelevant.
Reinvent the wheel.	Seek knowledge from those who have succeeded in the past and reapply.
Knowledge is power.	Ridicule the barriers to knowledge . . . sharing is a must!

As you can see, this simple tool forces you to think about where you are today and envision an end state that is far more powerful and far more exciting for all involved.

✳ If It's Not Simple, Start Over

Simple doesn't mean your vision isn't powerful or even far-reaching. It means that it's easy to understand and easy to communicate to others. If it sounds as though a consultant wrote it, redo it.

As Tom Ryan, the recently retired chairman and CEO of CVS/Caremark, once explained to me, "To get a message out, it needs to be simple and it needs to be straightforward . . . I think one of the jobs of a leader is to simplify the complex. And I don't mean simple from a concept standpoint. I mean simple from the standpoint of 'I can remember it.'"

Not long ago, Ryan's company came up with a new mission, which was "to find easy and effective solutions for our customers," because the health care business tends to be complicated, and people's lives are already complicated enough. But with 220,000 people in his organization, 45 percent of whom are part time, and a lot of movement in and out, he worried whether his message was getting through. Did people get it?

Then one day he walked into the cafeteria and saw a group of employees sitting at a table just outside the door. He had noticed that this same group of people sat at this same table every single day to have lunch. So he walked over to them and asked them why they always chose to eat in the same spot. Without missing a beat, one of them replied with a smile, "Because it's easy and effective, Tom. It's easy and effective." Ryan was thrilled. "I said to myself, 'It's working! People are getting it.'"

* Insights and Actions

Self-reflection

Assess yourself on the following items related to chapter 7, "Create a Vision and Personalize It":	Personal Opportunity	Personal Strength
1. I challenge my team to set Big Goals of their own and push beyond incremental thinking.		
2. Each person on my team knows our vision and can explain it.		
3. I use meetings and everyday interactions to engage, energize, and inspire others around our vision.		
4. People on the team are excited about our vision.		
5. Everyone on the team has personalized the vision and understands what he or she needs to do to make it happen.		

Exercise

Practice making the vision for your Big Goal as simple and attention getting as possible! Find someone to share it with and ask for feedback.

Is it easy to understand? Is it big? Is it compelling? How could you improve it?

8

* strategy: gain alignment every step of the way at every level

Once you've shared the business realities and your vision with your team, the third part of executing your strategy is to gain alignment. Alignment is hugely important. You can have the best idea in the world, but it won't matter if you can't get people onboard to help you make it happen. If you can't get alignment, your great idea is not an effective idea.

I've had the misfortune of witnessing firsthand how big notions can fail because of a lack of alignment. This is so important that you have to do more than just *think* you have it; you have to *know* you have it. One of the biggest mistakes I've made since I started running Yum! Brands was that I didn't follow through in getting *enough* alignment when it came to a big new concept, multibranding, which we were introducing throughout all our restaurant brands.

Multibranding is what we, in our industry, call restaurant units that encompass more than one brand—a combination KFC and Taco Bell, for example. The potential benefits of this concept were huge for our company. When we were spun off from PepsiCo, we owned three well-established brands, but each stood primarily for one type of food: KFC is about chicken; Pizza Hut is about pizza; Taco Bell is about Mexican food. Because the brands were so specialized, the consumer never gave us much credit when we tried to introduce different categories, like hamburgers at Taco Bell. If someone wants a hamburger, they go to Wendy's or Burger King. Well, one of our most innovative franchisees, Al Luihn, had the ingenious idea to try adding the Taco Bell brand to his KFC because there were no Taco Bells near his store. The results were fantastic. With just signage alone, no other advertising, sales jumped over 35 percent because consumers loved the idea of branded variety. If some in a group didn't want chicken, they could have a taco or burrito instead. Everyone was happy.

We opened more KFC/Taco Bells with similar success, but we couldn't make it a big national idea because we already had stand-alone Taco Bells and KFCs near each other in most trade areas. Here again, our franchisees led the way with a solution to the problem. Larry Durrett requested the opportunity to add Long John Silver's seafood to his Taco Bell in Texas. Jackie Trujillo had a similar idea to combine A&W All American Food, which had burgers, hot dogs, and root beer floats, with KFC in Utah. Again, the results were outstanding, so much so that we made the decision to acquire LJS and A&W in order to scale multibranding in a big way in the United States.

Even though our customers loved the idea and sales increases were substantial, I quickly learned that I hadn't done enough to get inside the minds of my target audience and bring along the franchisees. Those who had tested multibranding were passionate about the idea, but their early-adopter mind-set was very different from that of the vast majority of our franchisees, most of which were dedicated solely to their own brands. They couldn't imagine sharing their restaurants with another brand. It meant a new menu, new kitchen equipment, different training for the staff. It meant a commitment of time and resources for the owners and managers of these restaurants, and before I made the acquisition, I didn't do enough to understand where the franchisees were coming from or show them how big the upside could be for them if they made it work.

Gaining true alignment is key to ownership and accountability. On paper, multibranding seemed like the next big thing in our business, and a lot of people were excited about it. In fact, I even went public, saying it was the biggest idea in our industry since the drive-through window. But the people who had to execute the idea, namely the franchisees, by and large, didn't have their hearts in it. And at the end of the day, we were simply never able to make multibranding work in a big-time way. We are now in the process of selling LJS and A&W so we can focus on our much bigger growth opportunities.

✳ Beware of Slow-Nos

Have you ever presented an idea to a group of people who seemed to like it—at least they didn't raise any objections—only to find out later on that some of them were never really on board in the first place? You have to remember that simply giving a presentation on your plan is not enough. You have to follow it up by sniffing out those "slow-nos," the people who don't really like conflict and may not want to voice their concerns, but nevertheless, down the track, can kill your initiative.

If certain individuals are important in terms of moving your goal forward, you have to ask them directly: Are you on board? Have I satisfied your concerns? This is where knowing your people and how they think comes in. If you've got someone in the room who is usually against price increases and a price increase is a part of your plan, then you have to say to that guy, "Hey, I know you hate price increases. What do you think about this?" If you know the finance guy usually quibbles over the numbers but today he's being unusually quiet, call him out and get him to declare publicly exactly what he thinks.

tool: crisis-like collaboration vs. superficial teaming

Have you ever had the experience of working with a group of strangers in a crisis situation? Even though you didn't know each other, you might have observed that you worked together amazingly well because you united during a crisis. Welcome to crisis-like collaboration, a way of working together that leads to breakthrough results.

You've probably also had the experience of being part of a team at work in which, even though you see each other every day, you never get to know each other very well. As a result, when you get in a room together, you don't really participate fully and your collaboration remains mediocre. This is superficial teaming, or just another way to get incrementalism.

Crisis-like collaboration is different because, in a crisis, people:

- Combine efforts for immediate results.
- Build a strong bond quickly.
- May feel unusually close.

To get crisis-like collaboration, shift from the Have-Do-Be model to the Be-Do-Have model:

Have-Do-Be Model	Be-Do-Have Model
Must *have* willing partners	Resolve to *be* collaborative
Can then *do* reviews together	Can then *do* things together
Can then *be* collaborative	Will then *have* willing partners and results

This is the kind of teaming we want to experience every day. How do you generate crisis-like collaboration without a crisis? You have to start with a basic belief in people and their good intentions, then *choose* to collaborate this way, no matter what happens. Without choosing to do it, it will not happen by accident.

© *John O'Keeffe, BusinessBeyondtheBox.com*

* Three Steps Toward Gaining Alignment

To sniff out those slow-nos and begin making sure you have alignment, rather than just thinking you have it, start with the following three steps:

1. *Share the reality . . . help people understand the why:* Don't just tell people what you want to do, explain why you want to do it. It's the why that engages people the most.

> *Getting alignment is very important, and how I gain it is by doing three things: You tell people what, you tell people how, but most important, and it's something we're not particularly good at, you have to tell them why. Now, telling them what engages their head. Telling them how engages their hands. And telling them why engages their heart and enables you to make an emotional connection. And it's through an emotional connection that you get the best alignment.*
>
> —GREG CREED, CHIEF EXECUTIVE OFFICER, TACO BELL

2. *Ask for input . . . show that you've listened:* Ask direct questions based on what you know about your challenge, and then let people know that you heard and appreciate what they had to say. If you use someone's idea to make your plan better, give her credit. If you disagree with someone's assessment, tell him why. If you agree with Sally's concerns but don't yet have an answer for her, say, "I'm going to spend some more time looking into the issue that Sally brought up, and I'd love her help in doing it."

3. *No involvement equals no commitment:* Get your target audience involved, or they will never be truly committed to the goal. Think about any time someone has asked you to do something but didn't ask what you thought. How committed were you, really? I can guarantee that the answer is "not very" or "not as much as I could have been."

✳ Productive Conflict

How do you deal with conflict? This is an important question in terms of gaining alignment. How do the people on your team deal with it?

Most people dislike conflict. Too often, they try to avoid it, especially at work, where we sometimes don't know people all that well but are expected to be polite to everyone. But the road to real alignment is often paved with conflict.

Patrick Lencioni talked to us at one of our conventions about his bestselling book, *The Five Dysfunctions of a Team*, in which he identified a "fear of conflict" as dysfunction number two. He told us, "Teams that engage in productive conflict know that the only purpose is to produce the best possible solution in the shortest amount of time."

The first step in dealing with this dysfunction is to acknowledge that you, and many others, tend to avoid conflict as a matter of habit. Then realize that conflict can be productive and make an effort to embrace it. Expect to be challenged on your ideas. Remember to thank people when they do so. Let them know you value these kinds of discussions and appreciate their feedback. And most of all, never allow yourself or others to say, "Let's take this off-line." This is a major pet peeve of mine. When you hear that phrase, you know that people are just avoiding conflict and delaying decision making, which will never get you alignment.

I have to admit, I sometimes have difficulty practicing what I preach, which is what happened recently while I was trying to improve our weeknight business at Pizza Hut. Pizza Hut has traditionally been mostly a weekend business, with the majority of our customers choosing us on Friday, Saturday, or Sunday nights. We had introduced some new products to draw in more customers—Tuscani Pastas and Wing-Street chicken wings. Although our customers liked these products, they weren't coming in more often to have them. Instead, they were simply substituting pasta or wings for pizza when they used us over the weekend, so sales stayed basically the same.

I wanted us to do some promotions to leverage these new product categories and help spur on business during the week: Tuesday Night Pasta and Wednesday Night Wings. I kept suggesting the idea and became very frustrated that, while heads were nodding their agreement during meetings, it never seemed to actually happen. But my frustration was really my own fault. I never said, "Are we going to do this? When is it going to happen?" I never forced alignment or commitment. I never led a big enough discussion about the barriers the

You want to get to the best decision, the best answers, and in order to get the best answers, you've got to ask people what their opinions are. With my personality, for example, if you were to disagree with me, I'm going to probably argue with you. I don't want that to be a negative. I mean, that's the way I am, but I don't want that to stop you from setting forth your viewpoint in whatever way you want to. And when I had staff meetings, I mean, we had to take a break once in a while. Because everybody was yelling. But I think that's OK. Get the ideas and thoughts out on the table, and then sit together and see if you can make the best choice. Not a consensus decision, they're the worst ones, but the best decision you can make.

—LARRY BOSSIDY, AUTHOR OF *EXECUTION* AND FORMER VICE CHAIRMAN OF GE AND CEO OF ALLIED SIGNAL

team faced on its path to making it happen.

The team finally got the idea going and made it even better by figuring out how to do it as a value promotion: $9.99 pastas on Tuesdays and $.50 wings on Wednesdays. It took some time to align our franchisees, who were initially reluctant to take media dollars away from our weekend business to support the idea, but now our weeknight business is doing pretty well. In my view, however, it could have been possible to get it going a whole lot sooner if I would have gotten all the issues out on the table, including my own frustration.

As a final word on productive conflict, keep in mind that, as the leader, you do have to make sure you manage the debate. While avoiding conflict is bad, conflict that degenerates into pointless or hurtful argument is even worse for team morale. Let people get into it, but also recognize when some are getting uncomfortable or the level of discord has gotten too high. Bring people's focus back to the fact that the purpose here is to debate and *solve*. Your willingness to get things out in the open and take on the fight will differentiate you as a leader. It takes courage, but it's worth it.

exercise: encourage productive conflict

Larry Senn taught me one of the best tools I've ever learned for encouraging open and honest dialogue about someone's idea or proposal—asking whoever's at the table two questions:

1. What do you appreciate about what you just heard?

2. How could we make it even better?

Starting off with what people appreciate sets a positive tone for the discussion. It also puts the presenter in a frame of mind where he or she will be more receptive to the questions, concerns, and criticisms that follow.

By focusing on improvements, not criticism, following up with the second question encourages conflict avoiders to speak up. It also encourages those who tend to be negative to find a constructive way to voice their concerns. The question doesn't simply ask people to say what's wrong with the idea; it makes them think about how they could turn those wrongs into rights.

Senn Delaney

* Cascade Your Alignment

Alignment is a top-down commitment. It starts with you and your team. But then look back at your People Map. Are there secondary audiences? Third-tier audiences? Are there people whose support will be crucial, or simply helpful, even if those people aren't ones you work with on a daily basis?

To do this, you have to communicate broadly and never stop. Remember the lesson of Sam Walton from chapter 3: "The more they know, the more they care." When I visited Walmart, I learned that Walton had a knack for making a big company feel small because of the way he communicated directly with as many people in his organization as possible, by paying frequent visits to stores when he could, and then devising their closed-circuit television system for when he couldn't. One day he used that Walmart TV system to ask his store workers to be more attentive to the customer by greeting anyone who came within ten feet of them. He even asked them to swear they would do it by saying, "So help me, Sam." That phrase became a refrain within the company, a way employees could voice their alignment or dedication to anything that was proposed to them.

As a more recent example, the CEO of AT&T, Randall Stephenson, showed how Walton's maxim, "The more they know, the more they care," really works when he set out to convince his entire organization of the merits of his new vision—"Mobilize everything." As I mentioned in the last chapter, at the time, AT&T was full of people who thought of themselves as being in the wireline business, so Randall used what they called T University (because T is AT&T's ticker symbol on the New York Stock Exchange) to share all the facts that grounded the new wireless strategy and educate everyone on the technology and its potential. Randall considered this education so important that he had his top seven hundred people take part for a full week. As Randall told me, "We have a lot of smart people, and once they saw the same things that helped me draw my conclusion, they came to the same conclusion just as quickly as I had. It really got the top management of our company on the same page and ignited the shift in mind-set we needed to complete."

The flip side is that when we forget to think of *all* the people who will be affected by our initiative, we run the risk of unforeseen problems. Scott Bergren will be the first to admit that he created quite a snafu when, as chief marketing officer, he decided that the KFC Colonel was looking a little outdated and could use a face-lift.

Bergren got started right away on creating and testing a new image for the Colonel that made him a little younger, a little buffer, and a little bit cooler. "Over the course of a pretty short period of time," Bergren told me, "we created a very modern, great-looking new image. Customers told us hands down that this thing was perfect." The project got so far along that they were beginning to roll out the new Colonel in the United States when Bergren realized he had forgotten something: KFC wasn't just a U.S. business. He hadn't even mentioned the idea to the heads of KFC's international business units, who all had the old logo up in their stores. "You can't imagine what a mess I created," Bergren admitted. He had to go back to the beginning and present his idea, along with all the research he had to back it up, to those people whom he'd left out. It all worked out in the end, and now the new image is present in restaurants all around the world, but not without a lot of apologies and backtracking on Bergren's part, which not only lost him time but also threatened to damage his credibility with those people. "It would have been so much easier if, at the beginning, I had gotten alignment that the logo was outdated, instead of trying to explain afterward what I had done," Bergren said. "It was much more difficult that way. I just completely missed a step."

✳ Make Gaining Alignment Personal

Over the past twenty years, I've had the benefit of learning from a number of top-ranked change consultants. What they all have to say about alignment basically boils down to this: You have to make sure people understand three things.

1. What do you want them to do?

2. What's in it for them?

3. Are you going to do it too?

It's common sense, really, but as I said earlier (and I think it bears repeating), the problem with common sense is, it's not all that common. People will get on board with your goal when they understand it, they know what they'll get out of it, and when they know that you are as invested in it as they are. Only then will they truly feel accountable for doing their part to make it happen.

> There's an old Native American proverb: "Tell me, and I'll forget. Show me, and I may not remember. Involve me, and I'll understand."
>
> —TOM NELSON, PRESIDENT AND CEO OF NATIONAL GYPSUM

* Insights and Actions

Self-reflection

Assess yourself on the following items related to chapter 8, "Gain Alignment":	Personal Opportunity	Personal Strength
1. I involve my team in setting our goals so they feel ownership of them.		
2. I sniff out and address conflicts around critical priorities; I don't let issues fester.		
3. I know who the key stakeholders are for our challenges, and I understand their issues and concerns.		
4. I drive accountability with my team by helping them understand what we need to do and why.		
5. I openly share information with my team about our progress.		

Exercise

Seek out some leaders you admire and ask them the following questions:

- What feeds resistance in others, and how do you turn a resistant person around?

- What practices do you use to surface and manage misalignment on your team?

9 * structure: resources, organization, and process enable execution

It's one thing to say you want to do something; it's another thing to get it done. Once you have your strategy for your Big Goal, you have to put structure in place to make it happen. That means having the resources, organization, and processes you need to execute your strategy. These things together provide a solid framework that drives accountability.

For example, a number of years ago, we wanted to expand our lunch business at Pizza Hut. Customers loved coming into our restaurants for dinner, but they didn't see us as a viable lunch option for three basic reasons: our pizzas were too big, too expensive, and took too long to make. It was the opposite of the quick, easy, and affordable fare that most people were looking for when on their lunch hour from work.

To solve these perception problems, we put a dedicated team on a mission to develop the lunch daypart. The first thing the team decided was to launch a six-inch Personal Pan Pizza at a low price point. That solved two out of the three issues, but then we had to figure out how to ensure that our restaurants would be quick enough for the lunch crowd. So we put a process in place to make sure that customers could eat their lunch and still make it back to work on time. We offered a "five-minute guarantee" and put an hourglass on each table to mark the time. If the waitstaff didn't get customers their pizzas before that hourglass ran out, they had to give them a coupon for their next pizza free. Not only did this process entice customers, it also encouraged operational discipline at the back of the house, because it became very easy to measure whether staff were living up to expectations: Just count the number of coupons they had to give away. Our franchisees, even those who weren't thrilled in the beginning at having to implement a new process in their restaurants, were won over by the results. The promotion was wildly popular with customers, and we doubled our lunch business.

✳ People Resources: Building the Right Team

The first thing to do in terms of resources is to put the right team in place, one with the skills, knowledge, and capabilities to accomplish your goal. This is a good time to return to your People Map from chapter 1 and assess who you have working with you on this project. Do you have everyone you need to get big things done?

To do this, you're also going to want to think back to what you learned about yourself in chapter 2. What are your strengths? What are your weaknesses? Where are your blind spots? Too often I see teams of people who are alike. It's a natural inclination to surround ourselves with people who are similar to us, but that's not the best way to get big things done. What you're striving for here is a team of people with *complementary* strengths. As Sylvester Stallone said in his role as Rocky Balboa when asked why his relationship with his wife, Adrian, worked so well: "She's got gaps. I got gaps. Together, we fill gaps." Here are some ideas to keep in mind as you build a team to help you do big things:

MAKE A SUPER MILKSHAKE: I call a team of people who fill in one another's gaps a super milkshake. You get all these different people, put their personalities and talents in a blender, and what comes out is the smoothest, best tasting milkshake you've ever had. Jim Stengel told me how he did this when he was global marketing officer at P&G: "I know what I love to do and I know what my strengths are. I love to deal with consumers, I love to deal with people and concepts, I like to think big. What I don't love are all the daily minute-by-minute details you have to do to run a large company or function. So I put on my team people who were not like me, including a woman who was an MIT engineer and extremely detail oriented. I also brought in a woman from purchasing to help me revamp that system. I brought in a finance manager because I wanted more strategy there and more of a financial mind-set. So I balanced my team with people who I thought were right for where we needed to go."

There are really three things you need to think about when you make your super milkshake. As Jim summed it up when talking about the team he built, "(A) They had good chemistry together; (B) they represented the skills we needed to move forward; and (C) they complemented me really well."

REMEMBER, EVERY JOB IS A CHERRY: When I was head of marketing at Pizza Hut, I built one of the most successful teams I've ever led, out in Wichita, Kansas. In fact, it was the success of that team that helped earn me a promotion to run marketing and sales at Pepsi a few years later. When I started the job at Pizza Hut, people told me I'd never be able to recruit top talent to a place like Wichita. They were wrong. I hired people who went on to have top jobs at companies like Subway, Capital One, McDonald's, Wendy's, and JC Penney. I was able to do this because of the environment I created. We all want to work in a place where we can grow and learn. If you can offer that to others, you can attract good people no matter where you are.

David Cote, CEO of Honeywell International, started his career working at his dad's gas station. He told me, "I can remember him taking an absolute verbal beating from a customer, which was not my dad, and him just walking back to me and saying, 'You know, sometimes in business and sometimes in life, you've got to put your pride in your back pocket.' I can also remember him saying, 'Look, Dave, I run a gas station. They can buy gas anywhere. I need to do a great job on customer service.' It was my job to wash the windshields, and he made you feel really proud to do this great job of washing the windshield. It's funny how a lot of those simple lessons get lost when you end up in a big company." It may have been a humble beginning, but that gas station is where Cote learned a lot of basic business lessons that have served him well to this day.

You have to think of every job you're offering as a cherry and not settle for less than the best. In other words, every job is an opportunity for someone great to learn and thrive in that position. Too many leaders end up with just so-so talent on their teams because they don't know how to inspire, how to create a growth environment, or how to invest in their people. But if you're one of the leaders who does these things, then you can attract the very best people and expect greatness from them.

Your ability as a leader to attract, develop, and retain people is fundamental to your success. When you get your team right, you're going to get results.

tool: get whole-brained

Another way to think about your team is to consider whether, collectively, the team is "whole-brained." The two hemispheres of the human brain are responsible for different functions and ways of thinking:

Left brain: logic, analysis, order

Right brain: pictures, emotion, feelings

Many individuals tend to use one side of their brain more than the other. We call creative thinkers right-brained, while others are more left-brained. But in order to get the best all-around perspective on your business, you want a team of people who represent all aspects of the brain. When building a team, be sure to include both left- and right-brain thinkers. Look for people who think differently and have complementary rather than similar strengths and experiences.

© *John O'Keeffe, BusinessBeyondtheBox.com*

✳ Understand and Motivate Your Team

Once you have the right team in place, you have to know how to motivate them. The more you can get inside the heads of your team members, the better able you'll be to influence the team in a positive way. Below are three steps for understanding what will motivate your team members.

1. Ask questions that promote insight: If you want to find out what your team members are thinking, the best way to begin is by asking questions. My favorite things to ask are: (1) What's working? (2) What's not? (3) What would you do if you were me? In my case, these questions have led to a lot of feedback about our need to do more to improve restaurant operations. As a result, I recently put together a team to study companies that are known to be great operators. We've taken what we learned and are now launching a World Class Operations initiative around the globe. A number of people have also told me that they'd like to know more about what our brands are doing in other countries, so I started a blog in which I share in real time what I experience during my visits around the world, including pictures of the restaurants, people, and unique features of each location. Moreover, when I respond to feedback by doing things differently, I always point out that "you asked for it, you got it" to show I value people's input.

2. Listen for understanding: The most powerful way to motivate people is to really listen to them with your full attention and an open mind. When I'm about to ask someone what she thinks about something, I always try to remind myself to suspend judgment until I've heard her out. The worst thing you can do is squash a person's idea before you've thought it through. I think this gets harder the more experience you have. The more we know, the more we have a tendency to react by saying things like "We've tried that already" or "That's been done before." But

saying things like that are a sure way to kill someone's desire to speak openly to you about her ideas or opinions. Building a reputation for being the kind of person who truly listens before making decisions is fundamental to having a legion of followers.

3. Take note of differences in style: You can diagnose this yourself, or you can use readily available "style preference" inventory tools, such as Meyers Briggs, DISC (directive, influencing, supporting, contemplative), ProScan PDP Behavior Assessment, or LSI (lifestyles inventory), to help you better understand the individuals on your team. If you doubt the merit of tools like these, consider this story told to me by Jennifer Munro, president of EagleVision Performance Solutions. She used the PDP ProScan Program to help a CEO find a replacement for his company's president. After assessing his staff, Munro told him that the only person who really met his criteria for the job was his current secretary. "He was not very pleased with that opinion at first," Munro told me, "but then he started to pay attention to her work and gave her more and more challenges. She accomplished everything he gave her and enjoyed her expanding role." The CEO continued to give her more responsibility and within four years she had moved up to vice president, then executive vice president, and then COO. Today she's CEO of one of the most successful banking groups in her state. Sometimes these tools can help us see potential in people that we might otherwise miss.

* Organize Your Resources

How often have you heard someone articulate a goal or a vision in business but then not put resources to achieve it? What does that say to you? It signals that the goal was never really a top priority in the first place.

It's dangerous when this happens, for two reasons: (1) A lack of resources put toward a goal gives people permission not to focus on it, and (2) The next time you have a goal you want to accomplish, your people may wonder if you're just crying wolf. You say this is important, but you said that the last time, when you didn't back it up. If you don't organize your resources around making something happen, how can you expect people to take you seriously? Conversely, if you put in place what is needed to accomplish your Big Goal, you get rid of all the excuses for why it can't be done.

It's simply a matter of putting your money (and your people) where your mouth is to show what's important. Here are some examples of how you might need to organize your resources to achieve your Big Goal.

CREATE NEW ROLES: At Pizza Hut, our Yum! Restaurants International CEO, Graham Allan, wanted to build our business in casual dining and specialty beverages, like smoothies, coffees, and teas, but we didn't have enough knowledge in these areas. To fix that, Graham recruited people from outside the organization who had such expertise, including someone who had helped develop a very successful beverage program for one of our competitors.

DEFINE ROLES MORE CLEARLY: Not long ago, we decided at Yum! that we needed to decentralize some of our functions, giving responsibility for them to the brands themselves instead of handling them at the corporate office. But we didn't want this restructuring to demotivate or confuse anyone, so our chief people officer, Anne Byerlein, came up with what we call our Six Pillars of Yum! These spell out the main responsibilities of our corporate office as clearly as possible, grouping them under six headings: corporate strategy, public company responsibilities, performance management, know-how building for systemwide innovation, talent development, and culture design and evolution.

CENTRALIZE RESOURCES: Over the past several years, Yum! has been developing a new Chinese fast-food concept in China called East Dawning. One of the problems that kept coming up, however, was that there was too much variation in products from restaurant to restaurant

> *One of the most important things you do in any big company is, you need to be a catalyst on resources. I mean, we made the decision to just add one thousand more sales reps in China. And if I had waited for everybody to do bottoms-up budgeting, it would take us five years to do that. . . . We needed to move faster, and I needed to use my checkbook and my clout to make it happen faster. So I do think the role of any good leader is to be disruptive to your own organization when you need to be.*
>
> —JEFF IMMELT,
> CHAIRMAN & CEO, GE

and too much time spent on in-store preparation. So we invested in a central kitchen to prepare the food, which would then just require finishing off in the restaurants. This led to more efficiency and better quality control.

MAKE THE FINANCIAL INVESTMENT: Over the past few years, JPMorgan Chase has spent hundreds of millions of dollars on IT systems, which have allowed it to better communicate with its customers. The customer data gathered as a result has become a huge competitive advantage. On a smaller scale, at KFC in the United States, we wanted to push for better operations, so we spent money on additional staff to audit our restaurants more frequently.

Not only did this practice give restaurant managers more feedback on how they were doing compared with others and how they could improve, it also showed them how much of a priority this was for our organization, thus encouraging them to increase their own efforts as well.

* Put Process and Discipline Around What Matters

I was once in Las Vegas at a franchisee conference when this tremendous lightening storm hit. All the electricity went out in the entire hotel for a few moments until the backup generator kicked on automatically. But the backup generator wasn't enough to power the entire hotel. Can you guess where they directed that resource? To the slot machines. Everywhere else in the hotel was dark, but those slot machines kept right on ringing. That shows you in an instant what mattered most to that business. In the absence even of electricity, they kept the core of their business running by putting process and discipline around what really mattered.

A good leader understands what the core of the business is all about and puts the right processes in place to ensure that that core runs smoothly. Here are some examples of how other companies are doing this.

SINGAPORE AIRLINES: Their flight attendants are the single most important thing to their business, because they are the ones who have the most contact with their customers. So the company has identified exactly which qualities they want to see in their flight attendants and has developed intricate hiring processes to make sure they get the right people.

TARGET: Most marketing departments focus almost exclusively on reaching the customer, but Target's marketers spend 65 percent of their time communicating to their own employees about what the Target brand stands for. Why? As Michael Francis, their chief marketing officer, told us: "Ultimately what that has done is that it has created 315,000 brand ambassadors who really understand, not only what we're trying to accomplish from an enterprisewide standpoint, but how to take that and apply it to their own store."

PROCTER & GAMBLE: P&G had some growth problems in the past, but its leaders have recently managed to turn their business around. I talked to A. G. Lafley, who is a phenomenal leader, and asked him how they were able to do this. He said it was because the company had developed an entire religion around the power of innovation and they had

> *There's no point talking about inclusion if we don't train people to be inclusive. So we put in inclusion level-one, level-two, level-three training, and we made it mandatory. We didn't make it an option. Our experience was, people who are already diversity conscious are the people who take this training. People who reject diversity never take the training, so we made it mandatory. Everybody took the training. . . . So we put the money behind that, and I'll be honest with you, spending all that money up front paid off in spades because what it started was a movement.*
>
> —INDRA NOOYI, CEO OF PEPSICO

completely restructured to make that the focus. For example, they developed an open architecture where employees can share ideas anytime and anywhere. They also put in place a corporate innovation fund, so that when they wanted to pursue a new idea, they could do it right away, without having to go through the typical, drawn-out processes for fund approval.

YUM! BRANDS CHINA: In our organization, we've set a goal to make the restaurant general manager the number-one leader in our company. The reason is that RGMs build the teams that satisfy our customers. Sam Su, who runs our China division, has really put the processes in place to make this concept come alive. He said to me: "What does it really mean for the RGM to be number one? That doesn't mean that the person is number one, it means the job is of number-one importance. We know that we need to support that, so we structured everything around it. We were very specific about the area coach (the first line supervisor, who manages five to eight restaurants), how he spends time in the restaurant, and the next step up, which we call the district manager, what his job is, how he supports the restaurants. We have quarterly or semiannual RGM forums now. In those meetings, RGMs are the kings. And the function areas involved are there to provide answers, and they better have good answers, because otherwise there will be consequences. So we have all kinds of things specifically to support [the concept that RGMs are our number-one leaders] and to make it happen."

* Use the "Hit by a Bus" Standard

This use of the phrase comes from Jim Collins, who for his book *Built to Last* did extensive research into those companies that are successful, not just for a period of time, but year after year after year. One of the things he shared with us was that leaders in these enduringly great companies passed the "hit by a bus" standard: If you were to be hit by a bus tomorrow, would your team or organization be able to go on without you? Would they be able to continue to improve beyond where they are today?

If your answer is yes, then you are what he calls a clock builder instead of a time teller. A time teller has to be present to let everyone know what time it is, whereas the clock builder builds a clock, institutionalizing process and discipline around what really matters, so that people can use it to tell time themselves. This is an important distinction, because it's key to making your business stable over the long term. The time teller has everyone looking up to him for the answers, but what happens when he's not around or when he makes the wrong call? In my opinion, Hank Greenberg, the former CEO of AIG, is a good example of a time teller. The company ultimately collapsed after he left because he hadn't set the business up to continue in his absence. This wouldn't have happened to a clock builder.

These are the kinds of questions you should be asking yourself at this point. By now you've communicated your vision to your people and decided upon a strategy. In this chapter, you will have thought through how to allocate resources and put the necessary organization and processes around them to make them work. As a final step, ask yourself, Will that structure work in my absence? If you have to be there to keep things going, then they're not working well enough.

✳ Insights and Actions

Self-reflection

Assess yourself on the following items related to chapter 9: "Structure: Resources, Organization, and Process Enable Execution":	Personal Opportunity	Personal Strength
1. I surround myself with people who are more capable than I am in particular areas.		
2. I get personally involved in hiring the very best people for our team. I never settle for "good enough."		
3. I use every staffing opportunity to communicate the importance of diversity in strengthening our team.		
4. I constantly assess whether we are structured and organized to best accomplish our key priorities.		
5. I work to eliminate bureaucracy and process inefficiency within our teams.		
6. I ensure that follow-up mechanisms are in place around what matters.		

Exercise

As you look into the future, what stories can you hear yourself or your team telling about why your Big Goal wasn't well executed? Choose one of these stories and ask yourself the following questions:

• What is the gap? Is it a resource, organization, or process gap?

• What can I do *now* to close that gap and eliminate the story?

10 * culture: make "winning together" a big idea

the final part of your plan is your culture. This is a critical ingredient that many leaders forget to consider. Or they just ignore it. Too many people view culture as one of those "soft" things in business, not nearly as important as hard results like sales figures or financial returns. But having the right culture, one that breeds positive energy and success, is crucial not just to the success of your current goal, but to anything you and your team want to accomplish going forward. A great culture is what will allow you to get those hard results and get them consistently.

What is culture? I don't really like the word, as it sounds too much like a germ to me, but what I'm really talking about here is the work environment. As a leader, what sort of values are you projecting? What kind of atmosphere do you create for your team? Is it one in which people are excited to go to work every day, feel supported and appreciated, and know they can grow? There is a big difference between people working toward a goal because they are getting paid to do it versus working toward a goal because it is a rewarding experience. That difference shows up in the hard results that we all care about.

As I mentioned before, soon after our spin-off from PepsiCo, we did a best-practices tour of some of the most successful companies around at the time, like Home Depot, Target, and GE. A common thread among all of them, even though some very different industries were represented, was a strong culture that permeated all functions and all levels of the business. When we asked people at each of these companies what made them successful, they didn't talk about their operating processes or even much about their products. They talked about their culture and how proud they were to be a part of it. Numbers don't run a business—people do. And people need the supposedly "soft" things that come from a great culture to succeed. If you build the capability of your people first, then you'll satisfy more customers, which will make you more money. That's why culture is the foundation of any successful business or team. It's up to you to create a winning esprit de corps. It's the soft stuff that drives hard results!

✳ The Case for Culture

One of those early best-practices visits was to Southwest Airlines, and ever since, I've been a Southwest Airlines junkie. They were a perfect example of the kind of culture I wanted to create, one that put people first, was high-energy, and invited people to have fun while doing their jobs. The people at Southwest believe "Happy employees = happy customers. Happy customers keep Southwest flying."

If you're skeptical about the importance of culture to your business, just look at this one example. Southwest's culture is their competitive advantage. Consider the hard results in critical areas for business growth, like retention, recruitment, customer satisfaction, and ultimately profits, that stem from it.

RETENTION: Southwest has the lowest turnover rate in the industry, even though many of its jobs *pay less* than the same jobs at other airlines. That shows that people work there because they want to. Studies have found that two of the biggest reasons why people leave their jobs are because (1) they don't feel appreciated and (2) they don't get along with the boss. Those are culture reasons, not financial ones.

RECRUITMENT: In 2008, the company hired 3,300 new employees and received a whopping 200,000 résumés for those 3,300 spots. That's more than sixty candidates for each position. Numbers like that practically ensure that the company will get good people to fill every role.

CUSTOMER SATISFACTION: Southwest's customer satisfaction scores beat out every single one of their competitors' and have done so every year for more than a decade, according to the American Customer Satisfaction Index.

PROFITS: All this translates into a better bottom line. The company has enjoyed *thirty-six* consecutive years of profit growth.

> *The only thing we have is one another. The only competitive advantage we have is the culture and values of the company. Anyone can open up a coffee store. We have no technology, we have no patent. All we have is the relationship around the values of the company and what we bring to the customer every day. And we all have to own it.*
>
> —HOWARD SCHULTZ, CHAIRMAN, PRESIDENT AND CEO, STARBUCKS

✳ How We Win Together

At Yum!, we are becoming famous for our recognition culture. We regularly and publicly give awards to employees to recognize them for their good work. But our awards are not ordinary things, like a plaque or a fancy pen. Each leader chooses what form his award will take; some of mine have been floppy chickens (which I gave out when I was president of KFC) or cheeseheads (which is what I chose when I was at Pizza Hut). We also have a roving recognition band that plays when someone is being recognized. And those things are just the tip of the iceberg when it comes to how we recognize and appreciate our people. We went on that best-practices tour when we started, to help us learn how to develop the principles we needed to succeed; now companies are best-practicing us because of our recognition culture.

Building a strong culture wasn't easy, and there were a lot of naysayers in the beginning. When I first starting talking to people about the kinds of awards I wanted to give out, I was told by an executive in the United Kingdom that they just didn't do things like that over there. And in China, I was told that their structures were too hierarchical, their people just wouldn't understand it.

I stuck to my guns because I have always believed that people everywhere are similar in certain ways: They all want credit for their accomplishments; they all want to know that their work is appreciated; and they all like to have fun. I spoke once at Peking University in Beijing in front of a big group of business students, and this one kid stood up and asked me, "What makes you think you can come to China and impose Western culture on us?" I said to him, "I've traveled all around the world, and I've met a lot of people in China since I started coming here ten years ago. What I've found is that people in China like to have fun and be recognized just like everybody else." I don't know if he believed me, but I got a standing ovation from all the other Chinese kids.

Our recognition program is one of the things that sets us apart from other companies, and it's thriving all around the world, even in those places where I was told it wouldn't work. Shirley Kunamoto, who used to run our corporate restaurant support team, asked a Chinese restaurant general manager, Ying Ling, if she could see the Yum! award I had given her (that's my Chairman's Award, which is a set of smiling teeth with legs, for customer maniacs). She told Shirley, no, she couldn't see it, because it was so important to her she had it at home locked in her father's safe.

At Yum! we have come up with a list of How We Win Together principles, which are the foundation of our culture. Such principles should always meet certain criteria:

1. Are they relevant to your business?

2. Do they help make people feel as though they count?

3. Do they make your people happy to be working where they are, enough so that they'll ask themselves, *Why would I want to work anywhere else?*

4. Do they inspire your people to satisfy the customer and achieve results?

Read through our How We Win Together cultural principles, which follow, and think about how you might adapt them for your own business or team, or come up with your own that meet the four criteria above. Ask yourself: What am I doing to create a positive environment for my people?

how we win together

Believe in *All* People

We trust in positive intentions and believe everyone has the potential to make a difference.

We actively seek diversity in others to expand our thinking and make the best decision.

We coach and support every individual to grow to his full capability.

Be Restaurant and Customer Maniacs . . . *Now!*

We love running great restaurants, and our customers rule. We act with urgency to ensure that every customer sees it and feels it in every restaurant. We make sure we have great RGMs who build great teams. We are maniacal about rigorous execution of our core processes to deliver our Brand Standards as our #1 brand-building initiative. It's the foundation for making customer mania come alive.

Go for Breakthrough

We begin by asking ourselves, "What can I do *now* to get breakthrough results in my piece of Yum!?" Our intentionality drives step-change thinking. We imagine how big something can be and work future back, going full out with positive energy and personal accountability to make it happen.

Build Know-how

We grow by being avid learners, pursuing knowledge and best practices inside and outside our company. We seek truth over harmony every step of the way. We consistently drive outstanding execution by scaling our learnings into process and tools around what matters most. Breakthroughs come when we get people with knowledge thinking creatively.

"Take the Hill" Teamwork

We team together to drive action versus activity. We discuss the undiscussable, always promoting healthy debate and healthy decisions. Our relationships allow us to ask the earth of each other. We make specific verbal contracts to get big things done with urgency and excellence.

Recognize! Recognize! Recognize!

We attract and retain the best people and inspire greatness by being world famous for recognition. We love celebrating the achievement of others and have lots of fun doing it!

* Culture Is No Accident

A great culture doesn't just happen. It must be built deliberately. It's the job of every single person in the organization to create a positive culture and make it a big idea; it's the leader's job to make sure everyone understands that and believes in it.

How do you do this? First, you have to really know what you stand for. Next, you have to make it known. And finally, you have to repeat, repeat, repeat to drive the message home.

Here are some ways you can make your culture come alive:

CREATE SHARED EXPERIENCES: Everyone at Yum! receives the Achieving Breakthrough Results (ABR) training that I've mentioned before. The tools that are utilized throughout this book, courtesy of John O'Keeffe, are taught to every new employee at all our restaurant support centers. It becomes a shared experience for all our people within our very large company to have gone through the same training; a shared knowledge because everyone learns the same material; and a shared language because everyone understands and uses the terms from the program. Things like this are important to make people feel that they're a part of something. Another thing we do to build this sense of a shared culture is to periodically hold town hall meetings, which are an open forum for people to ask questions or voice their opinions about what's going on in our company.

KEEP CREATING NEW MEMORIES: You can't rely just on the shared experiences of last year. You have to keep it going and really watch out for those "I remember when" moments. When I was at PepsiCo, I paid a visit to a bottling plant that we had bought five years prior, and one of the first things I noticed when I walked in was a trophy case with plaques for Employee of the Month. The most recent one was from 1988. This was 1993. So I said to them, "Has there really been no one you wanted to honor in the past five years? If that's the case, you should rip out that trophy case, because it's really depressing."

The more I talked to the people there, the more I understood what had happened. PepsiCo had taken over ownership of the plant in 1988. Before that, there had been family picnics, holiday parties,

> *If we can compress that space where there seems to be this need for, I'm up here, you're down there, if we can just evaporate all of that into we, instead of you and me, I think there's no telling what you can unleash in the force of humanity by tapping into people's desires. Everybody wants to be a winner. Every one of us wants to have nice things said about us. Every one of us wants to go home and say "I did it." The challenge to us as leaders is to help people achieve those goals.*
>
> —KEN LANGONE,
> COFOUNDER OF HOME DEPOT

and so on. People kept saying to me, "I remember when we used to do such and such." There was so much nostalgia for the old days, it was palpable. And it was a huge problem. These guys had been so much happier working for the previous owners that it affected their performance. And really, who could blame them? To turn things around, I asked the plant's management to develop a plan for recognizing people every month and bringing back a family atmosphere, which they did.

It's the leader's job to make sure those memorable moments happen. For example, in 2007, we took our top three hundred leaders at Yum!, along with their spouses, to Hawaii for a week to celebrate our past success and to discuss how we'd keep it going in the future. People talked about that trip for years afterward. And so they didn't have to rely just on memories of good times past, I gave them something to look forward to. I made a promise that we'd come back in five years if we met our performance goals, which we have. We're currently planning another trip to Hawaii, with the same group of leaders, for 2012. Our theme is going to be Taking People with You to Build the Defining Global Company that Feeds the World.

CAST THE RIGHT SHADOW: No culture takes root unless the leader owns it first. So mean what you say. Remember, as the leader, you are always onstage. People are always watching you, so make sure your actions match your intentions. Model the principles of your culture yourself and recognize when you see others living up to them. Rob Savage, our COO at Taco Bell, gives an award each and every week to a different manager who has put the tools she learned in ABR training to work in order to drive results in her restaurant. He then lets all the other RGMs know about her success. It's a lot of work for him to keep up with this weekly program but the fact that he does it sends a powerful message. It shows that he cares about people and he cares about results and that he's keeping a close eye on both those things.

CHOOSE THE RIGHT PEOPLE: Jim Collins, author of *Good to Great* and someone who has researched the topic of corporate culture extensively, says great companies have cultlike cultures. And cultlike cultures are self-selecting. If you are doing it right, then when you build your team, when you interview new employees, when you review the performance of your people, culture should always be a key factor. You should always be thinking: How does this person fit with our culture?

As Collins explained to me when I interviewed him, "There's a very key question that comes up: How do you get people to share your core values? And what we really learned is that great companies don't try to get people who don't share their core values to convert to the religion; they find people who have a predisposition to those values, and they bring it out of them." It's for this reason that when I interview potential new hires, I always try to make it clear what we believe in. I tell them straight out that one of the biggest reasons why someone won't last in our company is because he doesn't display a belief in all people.

MAKE CULTURE THE HERO: Finally, remember to make a big deal out of your culture. When your team succeeds, point to it and show how the culture helped make that success possible. For example, when I hold a meeting at our Restaurant Support Center, I might recognize team members from the IT department for displaying excellent "Take the Hill" teamwork in solving a tough technology issue. Or when I visit one of our business units, I might recognize marketing team members for Going for Breakthrough in a successful new program. When I visit a restaurant, I might recognize someone I see delivering great customer service for Being a Restaurant and Customer Maniac . . . *Now*! I do this as publicly as possible, not only to make the people I'm recognizing feel appreciated, but also to reinforce the idea that our culture is helping our organization get great results.

It is critical that people know what you stand for in your organization. Before somebody gets hired, we sit down and talk about our credo. Everything we do in our business, we talk about it. We wouldn't start a presentation without it. I think it's critically important to recognize who we are, what we stand for. And it's really important that you have people who can rally around that. Anyplace in the world you go with J&J, you see our credo hanging on the wall, in any language, and it's what allows me to sleep well at night, because I know that all of our employees are really looking at the same priorities, the same responsibilities, and are doing things we hope in a way that we'd all be proud of.

—BILL WELDON, CHAIRMAN OF THE BOARD AND CEO, JOHNSON & JOHNSON

tool: where are you on the mood elevator?

A positive environment goes a long way toward helping people to want to *succeed,* as opposed to just make it through the day. As a leader, people pay attention to your every move, and our moods affect how we see the world, how we relate to others, and how open we are to new ideas. Senn Delaney uses a graphic model they call the mood elevator and staying on top of it gives you the best chance of making good decisions for your team and your business. So consider it an important part of your job.

the mood elevator

grateful
wise, insightful
creative, innovative
resourceful
hopeful, optimistic
appreciative, compassionate
sense of humor
flexible, adaptive, cooperative
curious, interested
impatient, frustrated
irritated, bothered
worried, anxious
defensive, insecure
judgmental, blaming
self-righteous
stressed, burned-out
angry, hostile
depressed

graphic courtesy of: **senn delaney**

Questions to Ask Yourself

1. Where would I place myself on the mood elevator at this moment?

2. Where do I think others would place me?

3. The last time I had a struggle with someone on my team, where do I think I was on the mood elevator? How might this have affected my interactions with him/her?

4. What are some quick things I can do to raise my mood when I catch it sinking?

5. What are some long-term things I need to think about or work on to improve my overall mood?

* Culture Evolves

Things change. Priorities change. The business climate changes. You have to let your culture change too and grow organically so it doesn't start to feel static and irrelevant to people.

We call our cultural framework our How We Win Together principles, but when we first started out, they were a bit different than they are now. Back then they were called our How We *Work* Together principles. If you recall the tool I introduced in chapter 6, "Tell It Like It Is," this change was how we defined the "second set" for our culture.

When we made the shift, we kept some things and added some others. In our first set we had talked about our belief in people, our emphasis on recognition, and customer mania. In our second set, in order to take the company to the next level, I felt it was important to add the principles of building know-how, going for breakthrough results, and employing "take the hill" teamwork, which come from a military perspective that the way to win a war is battle by battle, or the way to reach an objective point is by taking it hill by hill. (Refer to our How We Win Together principles on pages 151–152 for an explanation of each of these.) I also

Investment banking is a risk-taking business. It's driven by money. And it just didn't fit with our concerns about whether we were always doing the right thing for the brand and for the customer. So we decided to exit the business. We retreated, went back to the core business, went back to what we were—cards, travel, travelers checks, providing security and trust for people at home and away from home, and enabling them to travel the globe and do whatever they want. I mean, that's basically what American Express is all about and what it stands for.

—JON LINEN, ADVISER TO THE CHAIRMAN, AMERICAN EXPRESS COMPANY

shared with you how, along the way, I changed "customer focus" to "customer mania" to add emphasis to a concept I didn't think we had taken seriously enough.

The fact that cultures shift doesn't mean that you sacrifice consistency in your core values. Every culture should include certain firm beliefs that people stick to no matter what happens. Those are the things that will guide you in difficult times. For us, the idea that we believe in all people and put people capability first will always guide us. But at the same time, I've talked before about how you need to be constantly looking at the reality of your business and identifying the unfinished business. Doing this can affect the priorities in your culture. You can stay true to your core values and still shift your emphasis now and again to help keep people on the right track and ensure that you take your team to the next level.

* "People First" Doesn't Mean Low Standards

As a final word, I want to clear up a common concern that people have about culture: Having a culture that puts people first doesn't mean you sacrifice performance. On the contrary, being a good leader means that you are constantly building the capabilities of your people. And in order to do that, you have to be able to make tough calls about who is helping to raise the team's overall performance level and who might be dragging it down. At Yum! the bottom 10 percent of our people every year end up moving on to another company.

We don't draw a lot of attention to that fact because we believe it's much more effective to motivate people in positive ways rather than through fear of losing their jobs. No one likes to have to fire someone, but you have to think about *all* your people. What sort of message does it send to those who are benefiting the company when you turn a blind eye to someone who isn't? Asking those people to move on actually supports our cultural values, because the people who remain know they've earned their spots.

When I talk to other top executives and CEOs, I hear over and over again that some of the worst decisions they've made in their careers have been about waiting too long to replace people who just haven't been a good fit in their organizations.

In our company we take our People Planning Review process to heart because it helps us ensure that we are rewarding the right people and raising the bar on those who need an extra push. I personally review six hundred of our leaders every year, evaluating both the results they've generated *and* how they've generated them, meaning how well they've lived up to our cultural principles. Sure, you need to display measurable results to get ahead, but no one gets promoted in our organization until they've also demonstrated that they can help grow the capabilities of people they work with.

* Insights and Actions

Self-reflection

Assess yourself on the following items related to chapter 10, "Culture: Make 'Winning Together' a Big Idea":	Personal Opportunity	Personal Strength
1. I regularly talk about culture as a critical enabler of our success.		
2. I create shared experiences for my team that support and grow our culture.		

Assess yourself on the following items related to chapter 10, "Culture: Make 'Winning Together' a Big Idea":	Personal Opportunity	Personal Strength
3. I treat all members of the team in a way that makes them feel that they count.		
4. I work hard to ensure that my words and my actions are always aligned.		
5. I hold the team accountable for living up to the principles behind our culture.		

Exercise

When thinking of your Big Goal, how much time and effort do you spend on:

Strategy   ____

Structure   ____

Culture   ____

100 percent

Are you OK with that? If not, what might you do differently to alter your time allocation?

✳ Learning Download for Part II: Have a Plan

• Every leader needs a plan to get big things done, and an effective one has three basic parts: Strategy, Structure, and Culture. It's important not only to hit each aspect but also to consider them in order.

• **The best way to decide where you should be leading people is to start by fully understanding the realities of where your**

business is today. Then share that understanding with those you lead by telling it like it is. People will appreciate the fact that you trust them enough to be honest about how things really are.

• Imagine what the future will look like if you accomplish your Big Goal. You will build a better plan to get there if you start out with **a compelling vision of the future. And the people you lead will be more likely to help you make that vision into a reality if you let them make it their own by getting their input and ideas. Remember, no input means no commitment.**

• **You gain alignment about your goals and your plans to achieve them by involving people in the process of deciding what to do and how to do it, not by telling them what needs to be done.**

• **If you don't back up your plan to achieve your Big Goal by putting the right resources in place,** people won't believe that you really care about getting it done, and obviously you won't be able to get it done.

• **A culture where everyone wins together** is going to make it possible for you and your team to accomplish this or any Big Goal. To truly motivate people, you need a positive work environment, one where all members know they count and feel appreciated and respected.

• To further reflect on these lessons and put them to work for you, go back through your answers to the Exercises and Self-reflection questions at the end of each chapter. Next, answer the following questions, which will help you determine where you need to focus your efforts the most as you build your skills as a leader.

• What are the biggest aha's you picked up about yourself while reading the chapters in part 2, "Have a Plan"?

- Of those aha's, what are the two or three that, if you worked on them, would have the greatest impact on your Big Goal?

- What will you start doing differently tomorrow as a result of what you've learned in this section?

As in the previous Learning Download, the stories that follow are from people who have been through my leadership program and have had their own difficulties in maximizing their potential in a particular area. I hope you'll take some inspiration from how Cristina, Al, and Steve did something about those things that were difficult for them.

Cristina on "Tell It Like It Is"

I came from a company—I won't mention the name—where you absolutely didn't talk about bad news and where you would never admit your mistakes. If you did, you could lose your job; it was that simple. So when I came here, I had a hard time telling it like it really was, because I had been conditioned to sugarcoat things. But then, several times in meetings, someone would call me out, ask me if what I was saying was really the whole story, and if it was, could I back it up with real data? It made me uncomfortable at first, but it also made me think differently. Gradually I began to understand the power of being up-front and honest, of laying the problems out on the table *before* someone confronted me about them. Admitting to these things, though hard at first, gave my team much better focus. Besides, I believe people learn better from mistakes than they do from successes anyway. Instinctively, I think I knew that. But I had to make my behavior match what I knew. I'm glad people felt comfortable enough to bring what I was doing to my attention.

Al on "Creating a Vision"

My team was responsible for taking a new food concept national, but we were really at the nuts-and-bolts stage. It was going to take a *lot* of work, and it was going to be a pretty long timeline. So in order to get people motivated and emotionally connected to the idea, I presented them with this vision of what success might look like: "Imagine that, in two years, you're at a Super Bowl–watching party with your friends, and a commercial for our new food concept comes on. We've done such a good job of making this thing happen that it's worthy of a Super Bowl commercial. How would it make you feel to turn to your friends and say, 'I was part of that. I helped make that thing happen.'" They started picturing what the commercial could be like, who might be in it, what the hook would be. It really got them fixated on the result, and then it got their minds working on how to achieve it.

Steve on "Resources, Organization, and Process Enable Execution"

I'm a great motivator of people, but I'm not a good process guy. I've had to learn this the hard way. If I were in the business of building buildings, for example, I think of myself as the kind of person you'd call to oversee the workers and keep them on track. But unless you want that building to fall down, someone else is going to have to come up with the plan for the structure itself. I can follow plans as well as anyone, but I'm not so good at creating them.

As a result, I've worked for years in partnership with someone who is great on process and organization. I firmly believe that my career would not be where it is today if I didn't have him in my corner. In fact, I'd even sacrifice a promotion in order to stay on the same team with him. I know what my weaknesses are, and that has allowed me to appreciate someone like my partner, whose own strengths are so different from my own.

part three

follow through to get results

Our company did a study of the capability of our top three hundred leaders a few years back, and the area in which they overwhelmingly had the biggest shortfall was in their follow-through. I don't think our organization is unique in this way. Most people like the excitement of new ideas but then lose interest, get sidetracked, and fail to execute them to the fullest. But I'll tell you a secret: If you're one of those people who loves to start things but loses energy toward the finish, you're missing out on some of the most fun and some of the biggest joys you'll ever have in business. If you're doing this right and taking people with you, then when your team sees your Big Goal through to the end, you will have the privilege of being a part of other people's success. Sure, *you* will have succeeded, but so will everyone you brought along with you, and the pride on people's faces when they accomplish something they weren't sure they could is an undervalued reward in the business world.

To get the results you want, you're going to have to follow through with daily intensity. Jack Welch talked to me about "the relentless drumbeat for performance." A constant awareness of what needs to be done and the energy to make it happen are essential for any leader. What's also essential is that you hold people accountable for their part.

When I used to work for Steve Reinemund, who hired me to be the head of marketing at Pizza Hut, he had this little pocket notebook that he carried around with him everywhere he went. He wrote down in it every single thing that he wanted to remember, and when he took out that notebook and started writing after I'd said something, I knew I was going to get a follow-up call or note from him within the next few days. Jamie Dimon, CEO of JPMorgan Chase, is another leader who blows me away with his tenacity for action. He doesn't have a little notebook; he has an eight-by-ten sheet of paper that he carries around. On one side, it lists what he needs to accomplish that day; on the other, it lists things that people owe him. It's kind of funny to watch him when he accomplishes something on his list. He doesn't just draw a line through it; he murders it by completely blacking and blotting it out. Follow through is clearly something that matters to these guys.

Andy Pearson used to have a great technique for driving follow-through. At the end of any presentation, first he'd ask, "So what?" which was meant to get to the heart of the matter and clarify the main purpose of what had just been discussed. Then he'd ask, "Now what?" There were no purely informational presentations as far as Andy was concerned. That "now what" was his way of saying that you needed to follow up with action on what you had just presented, and he wanted to know what those actions would be. Andy understood that it was his job as leader to spur people on with challenges like these.

Larry Senn taught us something called the accountability ladder to drive a sense of personal responsibility. At the bottom of the ladder is the person suffering from complete obliviousness; he or she doesn't even know what's going wrong or what needs to happen. You move up from there to blaming others for what's not working. The ideal rungs are at the top, where a person takes responsibility for finding solutions to a problem and then gets on with executing those solutions. This is a great way to think of your role as leader: You always want to be moving yourself and your people up that ladder (see opposite).

When I took the job as chief operating officer at PepsiCo, I had held only marketing positions up to that point, so I knew very little about operations. In fact, I asked for the position because I wanted to learn more. I knew I wanted to be president of a brand one day and in order to get there, I'd need some operating knowledge and experience. So when I started out, I had to rely, not on my operating know-how, but on my people know-how. I was good at listening to people, at diagnosing problems when I heard them, and at finding the expertise necessary to fix them.

One way I learned was to visit our bottling plants and talk to the people there; not just the management, but the route salesmen and the warehouse guys too. One such plant was in Baltimore. We called it Fort Apache because it was located in the middle of a really tough neighborhood. It was the kind of neighborhood where, when you drove up, you could see bullet holes in the Pepsi sign out front.

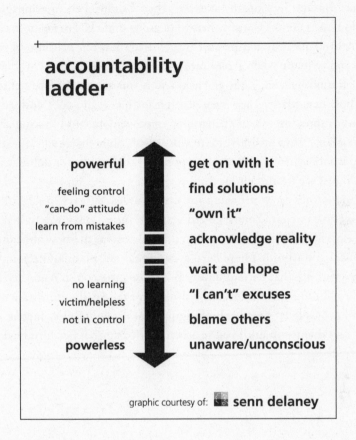

I went in and had my usual meeting with the crew. I started off by asking what was going well there. "Nothing," they said. "OK," I responded, "then how can this place be more effective?" Well, the floodgates opened after that. Some guys said they didn't have all the equipment they needed; others said it took too long to get the route trucks out in the morning. They just went on and on, until one finally piped up: "You seem like a pretty good guy. What are you going to do about all this?" That shut everyone up. They all turned to me and waited.

"Nothing," I said. "Absolutely nothing. You're the ones who are going to fix all this. I'm going to bring the plant manager in here and together we're going to make a list of all the things that you talked about. In fact, I've already started." Then I showed them the pages of notes I had taken. "The only thing I'm going to do is, I'm going to come back, in six months, and you all are going to show me what sort of progress you've made when I get here."

Six months later, I did go back, and it was as though I had entered a whole new plant. They were waiting for me at the door and led me around, showing me all the various improvements and talking about their plans. They still had more work ahead, but they had done a lot. And what's more, they were darn proud of themselves for doing it. You could just see it on their faces.

Sometimes the worst thing you can do as leader is try to solve all the problems yourself. You've got to assign responsibility where it really belongs. Even if I had known everything there was to know about operations, I still wouldn't have been around that one plant long enough to fix everything that needed fixing. But those guys could. And they did. Follow-through, like a lot of the things I've talked about, is leader led. You have to keep people climbing up that accountability ladder, and don't let them stop until you've accomplished all that needs to be done.

11

* market the change: be a bold ad for your big goal

What makes a good ad good and a bad ad bad? This is something that people in marketing think about all the time, but really, in this day and age, all of us are exposed to so many advertisements over the course of our lives, we all have a pretty good idea of which ones we like, which ones we don't, and why.

Good ads are emotional and memorable. They are relatable and address a need in those they target. They also drive their audience to action, to go out and buy that product. You want to see a good ad again and again.

Bad ads are forgettable. They feel irrelevant or out of touch with their target audience. They don't make clear what they're selling. Sometimes they're even so annoying that they make you want to do the opposite of what they want you to do. You never ever want to see a bad ad again.

As a leader, do you want to be a good ad or a bad ad?

Have you ever worked your tail off on something, only to have it fail? I hear this complaint all the time: I had the best of intentions, I worked hard, but it just didn't happen. To which I respond, "Did you market the idea or initiative? And not just once—did you keep reinforcing it until you accomplished what you set out to accomplish? Were you a good ad for your goal?"

KFC's founder, Colonel Sanders, understood the importance of being a good ad for his goal. As his chicken became more popular, he and his wife, Claudia, would travel around to different towns and put on

Kentucky Fried Chicken demonstrations in local restaurants. But they didn't rely just on the Colonel's tasty chicken recipe to make a good impression. Claudia greeted customers in an antebellum-style dress that cost the Colonel a whopping $135. And whenever he had the chance, the Colonel himself would come out from the kitchen in his distinctive white suit, which became his trademark, to do "a little coloneling," as the Colonel described it in his autobiography, *Life as I Have Known It Has Been Finger-Lickin' Good.* "I'd take off my apron, dust the flour off my pants, put on my vest, long-tailed coat and gold watch chain, and go out into the dining room and talk to the guests. Usually I had some cards printed up with recipes that had been favorites in our restaurant in Corbin. This would give me the chance to talk to the people and ask them how they liked the chicken."

You need to market your goal or your initiative in the same dynamic way you would a new product. You need to keep that goal front and center in the minds of your target audience. That means you need to get their attention, convince them of its importance, and *keep* convincing them. After all, you wouldn't show an ad for a new product just once and assume it had enough impact to go the distance. You'd replay the ad multiple times, then maybe do a new version of the ad to regain attention. I talked about how to create a vision in the last section. In this chapter, I'll talk about how to continually reinforce that vision— how to market that vision—in order to make it work.

6.5 seconds that matter

Howard Draft, chairman and CEO of one of the world's largest communication agencies, Draftfcb, told me about a study his company did that led them to a very definite conclusion about reaching the consumer: 6.5 seconds. That's how long consumers will give you, on average, to capture their attention. He explains, "That's all they'll give you because they're multitasking. They're on a computer, they're watching TV, listening to music. So if we don't stop them in the first 6.5 seconds— whether it's turning a page in a magazine, watching a TV spot, or another media—if we can't stop them with what the key fact is in 6.5 seconds, it's not going to be good advertising in today's world. I have to stop consumers."

Your target audience may give you a bit more time than 6.5 seconds (many of them work for you, after all), but it's still a good concept to keep in mind. Go back to one of the questions you asked yourself in chapter 1: What perceptions, habits, or beliefs do you need to build, change, or reinforce with this target audience to reach your goal? If you're thinking the way your target audience is thinking, then you can figure out what you need to do to get their attention. How are you going to bring what you want to get done front and center, so people take notice and give it their full attention? Be a good ad for your goal.

✳ Break Through the Clutter

In order to be a great leader, one who takes people with him, you really need to be a great communicator. That starts with an ability to gain people's attention. Be bold and be clear. When I decided that I wanted to make recognition a big part of our company culture, I didn't give away plaques. Why not? Because a floppy chicken is much more unexpected. It's also fun. I got proof recently that my floppy chickens did more than just get people's attention in the moment, that they had a lasting impact. I was presenting my Taking People with You program when a participant, Steve Robles, stood up and said, "I'm floppy chicken number 147"—because I signed and numbered every chicken I gave out—"I was working in Los Angeles, in the inner city, when you came to my restaurant and gave me your floppy chicken award. I went home that night and told my wife, 'Hey, David patted me on the back and said I was great. He gave me an award and a handwritten note.' It was magical, and the experience always stuck with me."

That was more than a decade ago, but Robles still sounded emotional as he described the experience and how he went on to get his

MBA and open several of his own restaurants, where he has established a recognition culture of his own. Do you think the event would have been as memorable for him if I had walked into his inner-city restaurant all those years ago wearing a fancy business suit and formally handed him a plaque? Probably not. Nor would it have made as much of an impact if he had stood up during the program and said, "I got a recognition award from you years ago." But "I'm floppy chicken number 147," that broke through the clutter. The whole room broke into spontaneous applause when he finished telling his story.

At Yum! we're dedicated to attracting top talents as soon as they graduate from college. But then, so are a lot of companies; we've had to find ways to break through the clutter there, too. Among our primary targets, we've identified young talent coming out of Northwestern's Integrated Marketing Communications Masters Program, and we've learned that one of their biggest worries is that they'll get lost in a big company like ours and won't be able to grow as quickly as they could elsewhere. Our strategy, as a result, has been to demonstrate that we want them to grow with us and that our top leaders are personally committed to that concept. We bring potential hires to Louisville every year, often by group in a company plane to show them that we believe they are the key to our future. We conduct interviews with them during the same day with all our division presidents, chief marketing officers, and me. We wrap it up with a special dinner that these same leaders attend, where I make a point of talking one-on-one with each person we know we want. We then make an offer within a week to show them that we are *not* a big company mired in bureaucracy (another perception a lot of people have), but that we can act quickly. We've heard over and over again that few places go to such trouble for kids just out of college. As a result, we have a tremendous success rate for recruiting Northwestern's best and brightest.

a good ad for a good cause

Maldives, a small island nation in the Indian Ocean, is the lowest country in the world; it is only about five feet above sea level, on average, and the highest point is just eight feet above sea level. As a result, one of the country's biggest concerns is global warming and the rise of ocean levels as polar ice caps melt. Maldives could literally end up underwater someday if the trend continues.

Maldives government leaders wanted to call the world's attention to this as a major concern, so they arranged a little publicity stunt. They held a cabinet meeting of the government's top officials, which was not so unusual, except for the venue—they held it underwater. The cabinet members wore wet suits and diving equipment while sitting at long tables placed on the sea floor to show the absurdity of what it would be like to try to run a country that was submerged under the sea. Camera crews filmed the meeting, which was picked up by AP and other news outlets, and the video went viral on YouTube. It's an image that holds people's attention and sticks in their heads, a great example of a good ad for their cause. So much better than a press release.

* Go Public So You Can't Go Back

Going public with what you want to accomplish is a great way to give yourself that extra motivation to see it through. Why? Because if you don't succeed, everyone will know it. You'll lose credibility and risk seeming ineffectual. To be a good leader, you have to put pressure on yourself, so if it's important to you to get something done, take a public stand on it. Going public will also give your people purpose. It will show them what you really care about.

President Kennedy went public with a bold challenge before a joint session of Congress in 1961: "I believe that this nation should commit itself to achieving the goal, before this decade is out, of landing a man on the moon and returning him safely to earth." We all know that it ended up happening, but do you know when? In July of 1969, just a

The business had just gone through a really significant period of growth. It had doubled in size the previous eighteen months. Unfortunately, it was losing a lot of money because we didn't have the processes in place to manage that sort of program. I realized after six months that while people's minds were fully committed to the strategy, in their hearts they weren't necessarily there because I hadn't given them the resources and means to do what we needed them to do. So I decided to make a big step in the form of a public commitment about how we were going to grow the business and make the changes we needed to make. And that chance was called People First, inspired by our credo, which is people capability first, satisfy customers, sales and profits will follow. I decided I needed to go public on that, first of all so that I'd have no way of turning back, secondly so that people would trust me and they would come along with me.

—IVAN SCHOFIELD, GM FRANCE, YUM! RESTAURANTS INTERNATIONAL

few months shy of the deadline Kennedy had challenged NASA to meet. That shows you the power of going public with bold and specific goals. It all played out just the way the president proposed, down to the timeline.

Not all of us have Congress or the news media to go public to, but the same tactic works in business too. Going public to your team is just the first step. To really go public, you have to tell everyone who will listen, your boss, your whole company, your whole community if it's appropriate. Going public to your team will make it more likely that *you* will give it your best effort, but going public *with* your team in front of the whole division, company, or community will hold the feet of the whole group to the fire.

When we first started our company, I sent out a personal letter to all employees to be delivered at the beginning of the new year. The fact that I handwrote it and sent it to their homes during a holiday break was an effort to break through the clutter, but it was also my way of going public with what I envisioned for our company's future, not just to employees, but to their entire families. If something is delivered to your home, your wife or husband is probably going to ask what it is. Your kids may even be curious. And they might even ask, a few months down the road, how much progress has been made toward realizing those goals.

This tactic works with personal goals too. Someone in our organization decided she wanted to run a marathon, so the first thing she did was start telling people about it. Then people started asking her how her training was going, which pushed her to train harder so she'd have something good to tell them the next time they asked. And when she finally got to the day of the marathon, she had a bunch of people rooting for her. Putting your goals out there will affect the way you think about them. There will be more urgency, and they will be more top-of-mind, which means you'll more actively seek out solutions.

tool: staircase of commitment

Anytime you want to accomplish something, think about how you can build your intentionality toward getting it done. Climb the following stairs one by one to increase your commitment:

1. Think you will do something and decide when you'll complete it.

2. Write down that you will do it and by when.

3. Tell others you will do it and by when. (Notice that this is when you go public!)

4. Listen for others talking about your commitment.

Use this tool to increase not just your own, but also your team members' commitment toward achieving a goal.

© John O'Keeffe, BusinessBeyondtheBox.com

✳ Shock the System

When you're going public with your goals, don't just tell people what you want to happen—show them. Once you've gotten people's attention, follow up by demonstrating the change you want. Howard Draft's "6.5 seconds" study makes for a great emotional word picture, but what's even better is that he had that number printed all over the walls of his headquarters. I talked about how emotional word pictures can help you communicate a vision in chapter 7, but they can also help you continue to market it.

I do something similar to reinforce our company's promise to put people capability first by lining my office walls with pictures. Pretty much every time I recognize someone, a picture is taken, so I have them framed and put up. When my walls started to fill up, I just kept going, expanding onto the ceiling against the wishes of our loss prevention folks who were afraid things would fall on my head or, worse, someone else's. (You'll be happy to know, we secured the frames tightly, and so far so good.) The extra effort has definitely had the desired effect. Without a doubt, I have to have one of the most fun offices in the corporate world, and it was actually featured in the *Wall Street Journal.* It screams "people first" and recognition. When family members come to visit our offices, they always walk away amazed and impressed by the fact that "he even has pictures on the ceiling."

Alan Mulally told me recently how he knew he had to shock the system when he became CEO of the Ford Motor Company in 2006. The company was losing billions of dollars, and many outsiders were wondering whether it could potentially go under. One of the company's biggest problems was that, once upon a time, Ford had stood for quality cars, but that wasn't true anymore, and Mulally didn't think his people were facing up to that fact. So one of his very first decisions was to take his executive team to the headquarters of *Consumer Reports,* which had recently rated a number of Ford models pretty low on quality. As the director of *Consumer Reports* started going through all the data, and Alan says there was a ton of it, his executives started interrupting to explain their findings away. Alan stopped them. "Let's write down everything everybody says," he told them, "because we're going to seek to understand before we seek to be understood." After that all the executives just sat and listened to the shocking assessment *Consumer Reports* gave them of their product quality. It wasn't much fun for anyone, but Alan believed it was necessary to shock his people into consciousness and prove to them beyond a shadow of a doubt that they needed to make some changes. And they did. In 2010, *Consumer Reports* rated several Ford models at the top of their list.

To give you just one more example, when Howard Schultz returned to his role as CEO of Starbucks after a hiatus of eight years, he decided that the company needed to get back to the basics of making great coffee and providing a great place to drink it. In his absence, he believed the quality of their coffee had suffered, so, as he told me, "To really demonstrate our comprehensive commitment to quality, we closed every single store and we retrained 110,000 people in one day." The move cost the company millions of dollars in lost sales but there was no mistaking Schultz's intentions. He wanted his people focused on making quality coffee, and he meant it.

* You Went Public and You Blew It. Now What?

You do have to be careful when you go public. You should work through the idea first and make sure you really believe it's possible to achieve before you start making promises. A bold announcement without a plan to get it done doesn't have a snowball's chance of succeeding.

Sometimes, even with a good idea and a good plan, things just don't pan out the way you wanted them to. That's what happened to me

One of the things I've learned is that one of the hardest things to do is to try to pretend that you did something right when in your heart you know you did something wrong. It's very disarming when you ask somebody what happened and they say, "I made a mistake." The conversation is over then, and you move on to, "What are we going to do next time?"
—STEVE BURKE, CEO OF NBCUNIVERSAL

It is not the critic who counts; not the man who points out how the strong man stumbles, or where the doer of deeds could have done them better. The credit belongs to the man who is actually in the arena, whose face is marred by dust and sweat and blood; who strives valiantly; who errs, who comes up short again and again, because there is no effort without error or shortcoming; but who does actually strive to do the deeds; who knows the great enthusiasms, the great devotions; who spends himself in a worthy cause; who at the best knows in the end the triumph of high achievement, and who at the worst, if he fails, at least fails while daring greatly, so that his place shall never be with those cold timid souls who know neither victory nor defeat.

—TEDDY ROOSEVELT

with multibranding. It had been announced as a major strategy for our company. We talked about it in the media, we talked about it to investors, we talked about it to our board of directors, and we talked about it internally to our employees and franchisees. So when it didn't work, I couldn't just pretend it never happened. I had to say something.

When these things happen—and if you're taking risks by pursuing Big Goals, they *will* almost surely happen—the best thing to do is simply acknowledge and explain. I explained what happened with our multibranding strategy to investors before they even asked me about it. But an explanation in situations like these is not enough. You also have to answer the question, "What are you going to do now?" In this case, I talked about our intent to focus 100 percent on our stand-alone brands and build new incremental sales layers with beverages and new dayparts, like breakfast.

If you fail, that's part of business, just as it's part of life. Don't sweep it under the rug. Talk about it with your team and diagnose the problems. Come up with a new plan, and then go public, both about why the last idea didn't work and about how the new one will be different. It's the best way to save your credibility.

✳ Insights and Actions

Self-reflection

Assess yourself on the following items related to chapter 11, "Market the Change":	Personal Opportunity	Personal Strength
1. I work to find ways of breaking through the clutter with my messages.		
2. I use emotional word pictures whenever possible to engage and inspire people around me.		
3. I go public with commitments and don't back away from them.		
4. My actions consistently reinforce the message I am sharing with my team and the organization.		

Exercise

Shock the system! Consider the ways in which you will communicate your vision and write them down. The questions below may prompt some ideas:

- What is a common set of key messages that you can build into all communications?

- How can you provide regular updates to everyone on your People Map?

- How can you encourage others to spread your message?

- How can you link your message to other initiatives?

12 ✳ understand and overcome the barriers to success

i n the last section, I talked about how to gain the alignment of your target audience, but in order to see your Big Goal through to the end, you can't just gain alignment once and be done with it. You have to keep sniffing out that conflict and come to terms with the fact that there may be some people who will never be fully convinced of your vision, no matter what you say or do.

I've had some learning to do myself in this area, even after I started giving my Taking People with You program. At this point, I used to talk about how you have to have courage and stick to your guns to see something through in spite of all the naysayers. But then, during one of my programs, someone raised his hand and asked me, "But what if the naysayers are right?"

It was a good question, and it brought to mind some of the biggest failures of my career, like Crystal Pepsi. If I had listened to the voices telling me the product wasn't ready yet and addressed their concerns, Crystal Pepsi could have had a real shot and might even still be on store shelves today. Those naysayers could have been my most important advisers back then, if I had just paid closer attention to them and adjusted my plan as a result.

The best thing about the Crystal Pepsi debacle is that it made me a better and more open-minded listener. People have saved me from myself over and over again during the course of my career. They have told me things I didn't know, stopped me from doing or saying the wrong thing, and helped me see where I needed to make adjustments to my thinking or course of action. In fact, I rely on certain people, like my chief legal counsel, Chris Campbell, to tell me things that I don't want to hear, and he does our company and me a world of good almost every time he does. I even changed this entire section of my program as a result of that one guy's insightful question. And the program, as well as my leadership abilities, are better as a result. Because, guess what? That guy was right.

I still believe it's important to have the courage to move forward with intentionality to achieve your Big Goal, but it's just as important that you don't do it until you've listened to everyone's concerns and considered all the potential barriers to success. This requires patience, maturity, and confidence in your own judgment, but if you do this step right, opening yourself up to the possibility that the naysayers might be right shouldn't lead to self-doubt. Instead, it will expand your knowledge and perspective, which, in the end, will make you even more confident about the path you're on.

tool: apply a powerful mind-set to the situation

Listening to criticism is important, but it isn't always easy, because we really don't like to be told we're wrong. In order to do this, you may need to adopt a more powerful mind-set.

Refer to the tool for Choosing Powerful versus Limiting Mind-sets on page 28 and think about how you handle it when someone expresses doubt about your plan or vision. Do you take in what people say and really consider it? Or do you push back, certain that those people are wrong or, worse, that they're trying to sabotage you?

Consider the differences in the mind-sets that follow and ask yourself which one is more likely to help you be successful. Always remember that this isn't about being right; it's about getting done what you've set out to do.

I might learn something new if I listen.

versus

These guys don't get what I mean . . . it's useless to talk to them.

They are trying to make sure we are on the right track.

versus

They are trying to undermine my authority and make me look bad.

* What to Do When They Say "It Can't Be Done"

The thing you *don't* want to do when someone expresses doubts is to plow ahead as if it never happened. But sometimes we do this without even realizing it, because we're so sure of ourselves, so sure that we have a good idea. The following is a checklist of what you should do to make sure you really are seeing all sides and considering all valid opinions and objections.

1. *Listen and understand why:* Take each concern seriously and get to the bottom of it. Why do they think the way they do? Could they be right? Remember how our general manager in France, Ivan Schofield, kept hearing that his plan for growing our business there was too ambitious? When he really dug into it, he understood that the doubts stemmed from the fact that they didn't have the right people in place to execute his plan. It was a valid criticism that made him rethink things and hire some new talent. It's important to adopt the attitude that if I listen to people, I might learn something new. After all, they might end up being right.

2. *Incorporate valid objections into your plans:* If you decide that the objections have merit, then it's time to adjust your plan. Doing this may take a bit more time and effort, but the result will be better for it. For example, when Taco Bell was launching its Frutista Freeze line of frozen beverages, we first tested the new products in three markets. Our customers told us they loved the taste, but our restaurant general managers in those markets told us they were encountering a significant problem with equipment capacity during rush hours; they simply couldn't produce the drinks fast enough to meet demand. As a result of their feedback, we delayed the national rollout we had planned in order to fix the problem. It wasn't an ideal situation, but if we hadn't listened and adjusted our plan, we surely would have encountered bigger

problems down the road when the equipment failed to produce in many more restaurants.

3. *Listen, then lead:* After you've heard and considered all the different viewpoints, you can't get paralyzed with indecision. It's up to you as the leader to make a decision about what to do next. No one wants to get mired in the debate forever, so commit to a course of action and move forward with conviction. When Bob Walter was taking his company, Cardinal Health, public, he came up with a very simple goal for the organization that they called the 20/20/20 rule. It described the straightforward financial benchmarks the company needed to reach. "You've got to grow your earnings at 20 percent, you've got to have a 20 percent return on equity, and then you'll have a 20 P/E [stock price to earnings ratio]," Walter explained. One of his most trusted advisers was elected by the management team to approach Walter and persuade him to lower his objectives. Walter heard him out, but then decided to stick to the plan. And it's a good thing he did. That simple but bold goal became an obsession for his team that they consistently achieved, which helped them build the nineteenth largest company on the Fortune 500 list.

4. *Do the right thing, and the right thing will happen*: Follow your instincts. If you know you've done right by your team, listening to their concerns and doing your homework on your initiative, then have confidence in your decision. Believe that if you've gone about making the decision in the right way, the right outcome is likely to happen. In fact, this is a good guiding principle for any aspect of your business. Nordstrom, for example, is famous for having a 100 percent return policy, no questions asked. This has to cost them a lot of money, but they reap the rewards in terms of customer loyalty. Doing right by their customers has made them legendary for their service.

* Tactic: Flip the Script

When someone says, "It can't be done," Scott Bergren, CEO of Pizza Hut, uses a technique he calls the flip. After listening to the person's objection, he asks, "What would *you* do to solve that problem?" This question drives home the idea that doing nothing is not the answer; instead people should work together to find solutions.

I once heard a story about architect I. M. Pei's using this same technique to get the unusual, triangle-shaped East Building of the National Gallery of Art in Washington, D.C., built just the way he envisioned it. He designed the museum with such an acute angle in one part that the engineers and stonemasons working to construct it told him that an angle like that had never been done before because it just wasn't possible. So Pei did the flip on them and asked how *they* would solve the problem. They didn't have an answer offhand, but they did work together to figure it out. Now that angle is one of the most notable aspects of the museum, and visitors frequently walk over just to touch it. What's more, the building has won numerous awards as a result of the team effort.

* Having the Courage of Your Convictions

You need to listen to the concerns of your target audience with your mind open to the possibility that they might be right, but when making a decision about how to move forward, you also have to consider the fact that they might *not* be. A few years ago, I read David McCullough's biography of Harry Truman and learned more about the fact that practically no one thought he would win his bid for reelection in 1948 against the popular Republican candidate, Thomas E. Dewey. Every media outlet that mattered predicted his loss, and one respected sampler of public opinion announced that his organization would stop polling, because the outcome was such a sure thing. Famously, the front page of the *Chicago Tribune* even sported the banner headline DEWEY DEFEATS TRUMAN in big bold letters on the day after the election because they had had the paper printed before all the results were in. Of course, they were all wrong. The story makes me think about what a loss it would have been if Truman had not followed his own gut instincts.

The idea here is to not cave in to people's ideas to make them feel validated or to avoid conflict. Instead, you need to seriously consider what people are saying and then make the right call. My great friend, my mentor, and the cofounder of Home Depot, Ken Langone, found himself in this sort of position in 2003 when he became entangled in a lawsuit brought by New York attorney general Eliot Spitzer. Spitzer claimed that the CEO of the New York Stock Exchange, Dick Grasso, had received excessive compensation when he was paid $187.5 million for his position and that Ken, as head of the exchange's compensation committee, had played a role by misleading the board about Grasso's pay package.

Many people close to Ken encouraged him to settle the case, especially as it dragged on for nearly five years, but Ken stuck to his guns against tremendous pressure. He did it, first off, because he believed Grasso had been an exceptional leader. Just a couple of years before the lawsuit, Grasso had been widely praised for his quick reopening of the exchange in the aftermath of September 11. Second and more important, Ken simply believed he'd done no wrong. As he explained to me, "[Grasso] was part of a system that was created twenty years before I, or that board, showed up. It turned out that Dick was there for thirty-seven years and by virtue of that longevity, his formula kicked in big time for him. But there wasn't a person that sat on that board that wasn't apprised extensively on his pay. And every single time that Dick Grasso's pay package was voted on, it was always a unanimous vote."

People may have different points of view about whether Grasso was overpaid, but there's no doubt that Ken followed his conscience. When it was all over and the claims against him and Grasso had been thrown out by an appellate court, he told me, "First of all, I had to live with myself. I had to look at myself in the mirror every morning and say, at a point in time when the bullets were flying, did you stand up to be counted? Now that sounds altruistic, but that's the way I am."

* If You Don't Have the Courage, Find It

Ken Langone knew instinctively what he needed to do despite advice he was getting to the contrary, but it's not always the case that we're so sure of ourselves. If you don't have full faith in your decision, then you have to do whatever is necessary to gain confidence. Before Indra Nooyi became CEO of PepsiCo, she made the bold decision to do a major overhaul of the company's IT systems. It was a $1 billion project, and there were a lot of skeptics. People weren't just saying it couldn't be done; they were saying she was downright crazy to even attempt it.

Indra knew she had to make very certain she was doing the right thing, so over her holiday break, she studied the problem from every angle. In fact, the word *studied* hardly explains what she did. In her own words:

> I bought 10 books on ERP, IT, data warehouse, all of this stuff, and read, cover to cover, these textbooks. I had some professors on call who were all available to me through the Christmas and New Year's holidays every time I needed clarification or had questions to be answered. IBM had done an architecture study for us and for each of the studies, the binder was inches thick. The IT guys dropped them off in my office, thinking I wouldn't read them. I read both binders cover to cover and made notes on as many pages as I could just to send the message, "Guys, I'm going to read this stuff because I'm not going to commit $1 billion of the company's money unless I know what we're committing it to." So I overpowered [the skeptics] through knowledge and competence, and I concluded after that that we had no choice but to replace the IT systems. And I never regret that decision I made. The team doesn't regret it either.

Be wary of anyone who says they're absolutely sure of the outcome before they've even gotten a chance to work it through (and that includes you). All any of us can do is make the right call in the moment with as much information as we can gather. If you've done this step right by listening to and addressing all the concerns and gaining any additional know-how required to answer the skeptics, then it's time to move ahead with intentionality. Your plan can be further tweaked along the way if necessary, but no one will ever really know the outcome until you've all given it your best shot.

* Cynics Must Go

Once a decision has been made about which objections to incorporate into your plan and how, then you should expect your team, even the naysayers, to put their opinions aside and work together with full effort and attention. Until you get some data from the marketplace that tells you it's time to rethink things, it should be full steam ahead for everyone.

> *Anything can be done. The issue is never that you can't do it. It's how much does it cost, how long is it going to take, and what are the resources? It's what do you have to stop to get it done? I mean, you can do anything.*
>
> —TOM RYAN, RETIRED CHAIRMAN AND CEO OF CVS/CAREMARK

If that's not what happens, then it may be time to get rid of those whom advertising genius David Ogilvy called "sad dogs who spread gloom." Positive energy will lift your team members up; negative energy will bring them down. I once heard a great analogy for this kind of situation: If a flashlight has one bad battery, it ruins the effectiveness of the entire instrument. You have to replace that bad battery before the other batteries can do their job. By the same token, if someone continues to be negative about your initiative in a way that is bringing down your team, he or she needs to work someplace else.

Whenever I go into a new leadership situation, I always look for the person that everybody wants fired and then I fire him. I've found that the best way to show people that things are going to be different is to get rid of the person who is difficult to be around, who is not displaying the values of the company, and who is not the kind of person you

You owe it to the organization to always listen to those people and to their point of view, because guess what? They may be right. So you can't be dismissive of that. But what I've found is that there tends to be a pattern. The naysayers tend to be the naysayers, and pretty soon you say to yourself as you're coming up with a new initiative, "I know Ted's not going to like this." You can debate it and have an open and clear discussion, but at the end of the day, a decision has to be made. And when you finally make a decision, you say to the naysayers, "The train's getting ready to leave the station and I really hope you're on it." Now what's unsaid is, if they're not on it, they might be happier somewhere else.

—DAVID GRISSOM, CHAIRMAN, MAYFAIR CAPITAL, AND CHAIRMAN, GLENVIEW TRUST

are looking for in terms of leadership. Doing so really gets people's attention.

There was this guy in our legal department at Yum! who was brilliant, but he didn't buy into our recognition culture; he wouldn't even pretend to participate. One time, when our roving recognition band started playing to honor someone receiving an award, he came out of his office and yelled at everyone to pipe down because he was trying to work. I couldn't imagine anything that would undermine the spirit of giving and receiving recognition more than that. He had to go. Everyone else was working hard to create a positive environment where people knew they were appreciated and wanted to come to work every day. I just couldn't have someone around who was actively working against that.

When I became president of KFC, I was also looking for that person to fire, and it didn't take me long to find him. There was a CFO who was so focused on making the profit plan, he proposed cost cuts at every opportunity, and people were sick of it. Every meeting, he'd come in with another cost-cutting idea—we should remove all the color from our packaging or get rid of the bacon in our green beans—and then he'd tell everyone exactly how much money that one cut would save us. Well, collectively, those cuts were undercutting our efforts to please our customers and grow our business.

Wayne Calloway, the late chairman of PepsiCo, came to town shortly after I started the job to check on our progress. Over dinner, I told him about this guy whom I really wanted to fire. "He's just so negative," I told Wayne, "always looking for ways to cut costs rather than build value. I just can't stand that about him."

Wayne asked me, "Does he know how you feel?" "No, but I want to fire him anyway," I replied, only half jokingly.

Wayne, who was a very wise man, said, "Well, before you do that, why don't you give him a chance to change. I know John. He's ambitious. I think he'll respond to some direct feedback." I was sure Wayne was wrong, but I calmed myself down and decided to do as he suggested. First thing the next morning, I marched into the CFO's office and told him I had a problem with his attitude, giving him several specific examples of what I meant. And then I said, "If you're going to stay here, I want you to wake up every morning and look in the mirror and say to yourself, as if you have it stamped on your forehead, 'I am Mr. Growth.' I want you focused on growing this company so we don't have to cut back on what we're offering our customers."

You know what? He did it. He made a complete transformation from Mr. Cynic to Mr. Growth. He really got behind our recognition program, for example, and even developed a method to expand it so it worked better, not just in management, but at the store level. Besides that, he and I became really good friends, which we are to this day. I still believe in replacing people who are getting in the way of progress, but you need to be a coach first, before you can make the right call. Otherwise, you might find that you've made a huge mistake.

* Insights and Actions

Self-reflection

Assess yourself on the following items related to chapter 12, "Understand and Overcome the Barriers to Success":	Personal Opportunity	Personal Strength
1. I approach challenges and push-back as an opportunity to make my plan better.		
2. I ask probing questions to make sure I understand all perspectives.		
3. Where appropriate, I incorporate valid ideas into my plan to make it better.		
4. Once I'm sure I've heard from all points of view, I move forward with conviction.		
5. I don't allow "uncoachable" cynics to be on my team.		

Exercises

Review your People Map and answer the following questions:

- Who will say it can't be done?
- What are their biggest concerns?
- Are they valid?
- If so, how have you incorporated their concerns?
- How can you either motivate them or move them out if necessary?

13 * use recognition to drive performance

recognizing the behaviors you want and those you don't is essential to keeping your people on track toward achieving your Big Goal. It's important to do this formally, with things like performance reviews and raises, but even informal recognition can have a big impact. I recently heard a great example of this while talking with the CEO of Ford Motor Company, Alan Mulally, who has presided over what many consider a miraculous turnaround. When he took the position in 2006, profits were in free fall, and by the end of that year, the company had lost a total of $17 billion. Just a few years later, however, Ford was telling a dramatically different story: In the first quarter of 2010, it made $2.1 billion, the best quarterly performance in more than six years.

Obviously a lot of things had to happen for such a remarkable turnaround to take place, but Mulally described to me what he believed to be the turning point. Soon after he took the job, he started bringing all the functional leaders and line managers from around the world together to review the status of all current projects, more than three hundred of them in all. Protocol was to display the status of each project on a color-coded chart: Red stood for serious problems, yellow meant progress was slow, and green meant everything was on track. But something curious was happening. For the first six weeks he was there, every single chart was green. Mulally told me, "I said to the team, I'm getting ready to announce a $17 billion loss and all our projects are green. Is anything not going well?"

> *I think that recognizing the wrong is equally important. Obviously to recognize the right is easy and good and everyone cheers. But sometimes it's also great to acknowledge that there was a defeat, something that went wrong, something that we planned incorrectly. And if it's used to your advantage for the next step, I think it can be very, very valid in the same way. Now if in a company there are too many wrongs too often, then it's another kind of issue. But really I think that in going forward, you always have to try things. Some are going to go wrong, and it's good to acknowledge them and find out why.*
>
> —MASSIMO FERRAGAMO, CHAIRMAN, FERRAGAMO USA

Two weeks later Mark Field, leader of their Americas group, showed up with a chart that was bright red, the only one in the room. Something had gone wrong with the Edge car in Canada, a mechanical problem that had caused him to delay the scheduled release for a week or two so they could fix it. Mulally described the room as "deathly quiet" after that, and everyone turned toward him for a response. He told me, "I knew they were all wondering, 'What's going to happen now? Is it really safe to say how it's going?' So I said to Mark, 'This is fabulous visibility,' and then everyone in the room started to chip in with ideas on how we could solve the problem. The exchange took only about twelve seconds. Then I started to clap and said, 'This is the kind of teamwork we need.'"

Things started to change after that. At the status meeting the following week, a few more red charts showed up. And the week after that, there were some reds and some yellows. The third week, Mulally says, "Three hundred sixty charts all of a sudden looked like a rainbow. I said to myself, oh my God, no wonder we lost $17 billion. On the other hand, for the first time, I really knew deep down I would be able to turn the company around because we were finally acknowledging reality." And to think it all started with one small moment when Mulally chose to recognize those who were doing the right things.

* If It's Important, You've Got to Measure It

In order to ensure that you are recognizing the right things in your business, you're going to need a system whereby you can track progress and identify when things are going well and when they aren't. People are moved by what is truly measured. What you choose to measure is a signal to your people as to what you care about and what they need to do to get ahead in your organization.

When I talk about measurement, people often think only of bottom line results: How much money has someone made the company this year? How much have they been able to cut costs in their department? These things are important, but you also have to track the behaviors that *drive* those results. For example, David Cote, CEO of Honeywell International, told me recently that they wanted their people to be thinking more about teaming, so they started measuring group performance and giving out team awards in addition to individual achievements.

In our company, we measure both the hard and the soft things, because we know that both sides are important. Our CEO of Taco Bell, Greg Creed, calls this being "smart with heart." The "smart" is the hard stuff like net number of new units, same-store sales, return on invested capital, earnings per share—the things we talk to Wall Street about. And the "heart" is the soft, which for us means 360-degree feedback, whether people are living up to our How We Win Together cultural principles, employee engagement surveys, leadership capability assessments, and so on. It's the combination of these two things that leads to sustainable results.

I learned a great example of the importance of measurement in areas outside of business recently when our company signed up for a health and wellness plan called Kinetix. The program's founder, Jamie Brunner, stresses the critical importance of journaling your eating and exercising behaviors as you lose weight and improve your health. "In the fitness world, the journal tracks our behavior and reveals our results," Jamie told me. "It allows us to troubleshoot when results are weak and replicate when results are strong." He says the journal is so important that he and his team can accurately predict clients' results before they even step on a scale, simply by looking at their journals. It's a near-perfect measure of their progress.

People need a sense of progress to keep them going. It's what keeps them on the right track and keeps them motivated. Jamie started his fitness program because, once upon a time, he was overweight himself, and without measurement, he says, he would have quit his personal journey. When he started out he was 300 pounds, and it was hard to tell that he was getting anywhere for all his efforts. "You don't see a lot of physical changes when you lose those first five pounds, when you go from 300 to 295 pounds," he explained. "Thankfully I had the data to prove I was making progress."

tool: d.a.n.c.e. model

Use this simple model to help you accomplish your Big Goals.

Desire—Know your outcome. Know why you want it.

Action—Take massive action to get to that outcome.

Notice—Notice exactly what you're getting.

Change—Change until you get what you want.

Extraordinary—Dance the extraordinary. (In other words, celebrate your successes!)

When you are in the midst of a project, the D.A.N.C.E. Model gives you the opportunity, at any stage, to check your progress and make decisions on how best to move forward by:

Noticing what results you are getting. Pay attention to what's happening in the marketplace. If the outcome is what you want, take this opportunity to recognize and celebrate progress. If it's not working, move on to C as quickly as possible.

Changing what you're doing until you get the result you want.

© John O'Keeffe, BusinessBeyondtheBox.com

✳ Making Measurement Matter

As the leader, you have to be careful that you don't allow people to confuse progress with success. Losing those first five pounds is important, but tracking and recognizing that result is only truly useful if it leads you to lose the next five and then the next five after that.

We learned that in our organization recently with our CHAMPS scores. I've mentioned before that, in some of our restaurants, we haven't done as good a job as we could have at satisfying customers. That's why I upgraded our culture principle of "customer focus" to "customer mania," to underscore its importance. But it's not enough to just talk about the idea. People really follow through on customer mania when we do a good job of measuring their performance in this area. That's why, in the late 1990s, we invented our CHAMPS scorecard. CHAMPS stands for Cleanliness, Hospitality, Accuracy, Maintenance, Product Quality, and Speed of Service, and each one of our restaurants gets rated in these six categories on a regular basis.

Unfortunately, that scorecard alone wasn't driving the kind of breakthrough results we were going for. Scott Bergren, who runs Pizza Hut, put it this way: "A funny thing happened over time with CHAMPS. We started to celebrate small movements in the scores, which aren't significant enough for our customers to really notice." This came to light when Pat Murtha, Pizza Hut's COO, traveled to a number of our U.S. restaurants to give a presentation on the importance of dramatically improving performance. He reported back: "Our managers just are *not* making the leap from the measurement to the result! They don't get that improving from 66 percent customer satisfaction to 68 percent is just not the breakthrough performance we need for our customers. I feel like I have to somehow recast our efforts so that we can really make a difference."

So that's what Murtha did. He decided to give some context to the measurements by dividing Pizza Hut restaurants into three categories according to their customer satisfaction scores. The top 15 percent were set apart as Brand Builders, the bottom 10 percent were Brand Destroyers, and the majority in the middle became members of what he termed the So-So Zone.

> *I can remember being an hourly employee and [the company] was trying to have this big focus on quality. We were only allowed ten-minute breaks two times in the evening and I said, "I'm going to check out this quality board to try to understand it because quality must be a big deal." So I'm looking at the Customer Squawks Board, as they called it, and I spent two separate breaks looking at this thing and trying to understand it. I could never figure it out. Nobody ever explained it to us. Somebody probably thought it was a great idea but no one ever bothered to ask, Does this work for you? Do you have any clue what it's saying?*
>
> —DAVID COTE, CEO OF HONEYWELL INTERNATIONAL

The effect was immediate. No one wanted to be a Brand Destroyer, so those at the bottom of the heap began to take action to fix what was wrong. The restaurants at the top were rightfully proud of their designation and therefore motivated to work hard to keep their position. But the most progress came from those restaurants in the middle. Being average had felt OK for many of them up to this point, but somehow being called so-so felt like an insult. The average performers started doing what was necessary to improve, all because of how Murtha had reframed their results. As Scott explains, "You really have to inspect whether the measurements are clear, whether you've focused on the few things that really matter for great performance, and finally, whether the metric itself inspires much *greater* performance."

* Are You Aiming High Enough?

As the leader, it's up to you to determine what success looks like, and you have to make sure you've got the bar in the right place. Back in chapter 1, when you were first setting the Big Goal you wanted to accomplish, I asked you to consider whether you were thinking big enough. The same principle applies here. When making sense of your measurements and talking to your people about them, are you signaling that you are happy with simple incremental progress? Or are you using your scorecard to encourage your team to go for breakthrough?

I serve on the board of JPMorgan Chase with Lee Raymond, the former chairman and CEO of Exxon, who is one of the most insightful leaders I've ever worked with. When I asked him his thoughts on this very subject, he cautioned me: "Measurement for measurement sake is not what it's all about. You have to think about what you want to achieve when you establish measures." As an example, he told me about the loads of data they used to gather on safety at their refineries. Each refinery would use that data to predict how many accidents they would have each year and then they would focus on trying to beat that number.

That was the method for improving their safety record for years until something extraordinary happened: One of Exxon's refineries unexpectedly reported zero accidents for the year. It changed everything. "This demonstrated that it could be done," Lee told me. "Traditional wisdom had been that this feat was impossible. But with that one refinery leading the way, now over seventy percent of our refineries have zero accidents."

This reminded me a story John O'Keeffe told us about Roger Bannister, the first person ever recorded to run a mile in less than four minutes. Up until that point in 1954, most people believed the human body just wasn't built to go that fast, but Bannister proved them wrong. And once Bannister did it, others followed quickly on his heels. Just forty-six days later, John Landy broke Bannister's record. And by the end of 1957, just a little more than three and a half years after Bannister had accomplished the "impossible," fifteen more runners had done the same. It's not that surprising, really. Others will have an easier time once someone else has shown them what's possible. These stories for me are a reminder that you shouldn't lower your standards just because something hasn't been done before. Just imagine if no one ever tried for zero accidents or to beat the four-minute mile. Measurements are important, but it's also important that you don't let numbers alone determine what is possible.

✳ Measurement as Coaching Tool

Once you know your measurements, you shouldn't keep them to yourself; go public with the results. Remember that "the more they know, the more they care," so make sure everyone you're working with has a clear understanding of what the benchmarks are and how well they're doing according to those standards.

Measurements can be a powerful coaching tool if used the right way. Numbers are hard to argue with, so they can help people stay focused on areas in which they need to improve, rather than feeling that they are being criticized unfairly. The following are things you should do to get the most out of this essential coaching tool.

> *I would argue that measurement gets distorted when there are too many. I tried to get the right set of metrics and as few as I could make them. And I don't mean to say that means there were two. But you ought to narrow it down to what those few metrics are, four or five metrics for example, that really matter, and then measure against those four or five metrics. I think people say, "Well, I don't know, so I'll add another one." You can't measure performance as accurately, and you confuse people by having them report on some stuff that may or may not be central.*
>
> —LARRY BOSSIDY, AUTHOR OF *EXECUTION* AND FORMER VICE CHAIRMAN OF GE AND CEO OF ALLIED SIGNAL

FOCUS ON THE VITAL: Measurements are no good if they're confusing or if there are so many of them that people spend more time sorting through them all than using them as guideposts to improving performance. A few years back, we decided to make our barometer for customer mania even simpler at Taco Bell. We'd learned that several first-class, customer-driven organizations had found a simple but effective measure to predict both customer loyalty and sales growth, which was the Recommend a Friend measure—if a customer is willing to put his own reputation on the line to recommend a product or service, that person was emotionally committed to it. So we decided to measure how often customers recommended Taco Bell to their friends and to make that measure a priority. We still collect data on each element of CHAMPS and turn it over to our restaurant general managers to help them pinpoint where they need to improve, but the Recommend a Friend measure is now the only measure we use to determine bonuses, which surely signals to our RGMs just how important we think it is. The new single-measure standard has some real advantages, as Tom Wagner, who started the program, points out: "It's simple, easy to understand, and easy to implement." And it has led to improved results.

CLEARLY DIFFERENTIATE TOP PERFORMERS: Don't cheapen recognition by doling it out simply because someone is meeting basic expectations. Doing so would be offensive to all those who bust their humps and overdeliver. When Larry Bossidy talked to our leadership team, he emphasized the importance of "rewarding the doers," which means rewarding those who have achieved tangible, measurable results. Who you choose to recognize has a real effect; it differentiates people, motivates them, and shows those who didn't get recognized what it takes to get ahead.

When my team and I visited Enterprise Holdings, the number-one rental car company in the world, I learned from their CEO, Andy Taylor, how they use customer satisfaction measurements to really differentiate and encourage top performers. At each one of their branches, they ask

> *We were focusing on the wrong thing. Instead of measuring the qualitative aspect of the experience, we were measuring transactions per hour, sales per hour, and those measurements started driving decisions. I think it put us in a situation where we were no longer delivering the qualitative romance and theater of what built the brand. And business suffered as a result.*
>
> —HOWARD SCHULTZ, CEO OF STARBUCKS

> *When you're in a group meeting and you have a problem with an individual who you think is either being unreasonable or not open-minded, it's important, right after that meeting ends, one on one, to sort it out. I think that's a big help. In a public meeting, you're celebrating success and all that sort of thing, but before it's too late and before that person forgets that behavior and that example, you've got to bring it to their notice. Sometimes people say something which they didn't realize was hurtful or inappropriate, and if you address them fairly soon, if it's live with an example and it's one on one, they really appreciate it.*
>
> —MICKY PANT, PRESIDENT OF GLOBAL BRANDING, YUM! BRANDS

customers to rate the service they received on a scale of one to five, with "completely satisfied" being at the top. I was amazed to learn that 82 percent of their customers give them a top-of-scale rating, which is quite an achievement. And to support their goal of keeping very high standards in this area, it is company policy that no branch manager gets promoted unless the customer satisfaction score of his or her team is *better than* that system average. As Andy explained to me, "When you think about it, we're not in the car rental business at all. We're in the customer satisfaction business."

TAKE ACTION WHEN IT'S NOT WORKING: Measurement allows you to see when things aren't working, which tells you when you need to make changes. I love the positive atmosphere we've created in our company as a result of our culture, but the other side of that is that I do end up having a lot of difficult conversations with people when things aren't working as they should. And I've had the painful obligation of firing a lot of people over the course of my career. We love to have fun at work, but it's also a place where you execute or else. You've got to embody both sides to be successful: Lead the celebration when things are going well *and* confront the truth when they aren't.

* Celebrate the First Downs

If you're doing a good job of measuring your progress and the benchmarks of success are clear, then everyone knows when progress is made, and that gives you the opportunity to celebrate your accomplishments along the way. And celebrations are essential. They are shared experiences that keep people motivated and invested in achieving the ultimate goal.

Years ago I was watching an AFC championship game between the Cleveland Browns and the Denver Broncos. It was an incredibly cold day made worse by wind and snow, a really difficult atmosphere in which to keep one's spirits up. With just five minutes left on the clock and the Broncos behind by a touchdown, they got the ball on their own two-yard line. It looked as though they were sure to lose. But then the team, led by Hall of Fame quarterback John Elway, started moving the ball steadily across the field, play by play, first down after first down. They got nine first downs in all before finally scoring a touchdown with just thirty-seven seconds left in regulation play. It was an incredible ninety-eight-yard drive to tie the score, and Denver went on to win the game in overtime.

It was an amazing thing to watch, but what caught my attention the most was the way the whole team celebrated each and every one of those first downs. The guys on the sidelines were clapping and cheering the whole way down the field. Research has shown just how important this is too: A recent study of soccer players, for example, found that the team that celebrated goals with the most enthusiasm typically won the game.

It's a great lesson for any leader: Don't

> *I never wanted to see a fellow score a basket that didn't thank somebody. Now don't run over and shake his hand or the other team will go down and score. But you give him a wink, a nod, a point or something. I had a player one time say, "Well, what if he's not looking?" I said, "He's looking. And if not, I will be."*
>
> —JOHN WOODEN, HALL OF FAME BASKETBALL COACH, UCLA

wait for the win or until you cross the finish line. If you just drill people about performance without pausing to celebrate the small victories, you'll wear people out. It's your job as leader to determine where your own first downs will be. If your sales figures were down 4 percent last quarter and this quarter they are down just 3 percent, well, you're not in the plus column yet, but it's an achievement worth paying attention to. Realize and communicate that you're not satisfied yet and you don't want to stay where you are, but take some time to congratulate people for moving things forward. That's progress, and progress is always worth celebrating. Now, I realize that some believe if you tell people "good job," you take the pressure off and they won't work as hard. If that's the case, I would contend that the real problem is you have the wrong people working for you.

✳ Insights and Actions

Self-reflection:

Assess yourself on the following items related to chapter 13, "Use Recognition to Drive Performance":	Personal Opportunity	Personal Strength
1. I measure the outcomes I need, both "hard stuff" and "soft stuff," and take action on results (celebrate or course-correct).		
2. I spend significant time planning and following through on the development of my people.		
3. I treat every interaction as an opportunity to inspire and coach others to provide their maximum effort.		
4. When I see performance that falls short of expectations, I don't hesitate to coach and, if necessary, take action.		
5. When evaluating performance, I consider both *what* was achieved and *how* it was achieved.		

Exercise

Take some time to think through *all* the things that show you're making progress toward your Big Goal. What are the numerical benchmarks of success for your particular project?

Then look back at chapter 10 in which we talked about culture. What are the "soft" things that create the kind of work environment that will breed the kind of success you want? How well are you and your team members doing in that department?

As a leader, how much time/effort do you spend focusing on and/or talking about:

- Hard Stuff: _____
- Soft Stuff: _____

100 percent

14 * the change is never over

this idea of your work never being over is true for your goal, and it's true for your business overall. As one of my board members, Massimo Ferragamo, said to me once, "If someone says that the changes are over, they are over. I personally believe that every arrival point is a departing point, and you have to always think that way."

Massimo's business is a family business, started by his father, so he's been in a unique position to witness just how true this is over the long term. When he started working in the United States, trying to make his Italian shoe brand popular in a new market, there was really just one major competitor in the ladies' shoe market and one in the men's shoe market. So his team studied every detail of those competitors, from pricing to positioning to incentives given to salespeople. He says, "We went after [those competitors] like they were our target. And the success story was that we beat them both by looking at exactly what they were doing and trying to do it a little bit better."

Massimo remembers it as a continual process of improvement to reach that goal, and they never stopped wondering how they could get another extra edge. But now other companies are targeting his and trying to evolve in the same way that they did. Less than a decade ago, no one was selling as many shoes in the United States as Ferragamo, but now the competition has just ballooned. "From being a company that was the leader out of maybe ten brands, today we have big fights to keep our position out of seventy or eighty brands. So the landscape has changed completely, and we are back in a position that we have to think the same way we were thinking twenty years ago about getting back that number-one spot."

Our U.S. Pizza Hut general manager, Brian Niccol, recently visited Google in order to gain some insights into how to improve Pizza Hut's e-commerce business. Brian returned with an idea that affected not just that goal, but his overall business perspective. He had noticed that on the Google search engine, staff tells users when they are in beta, so he asked about it. Jim Lecinski, a managing director at Google, replied that they are "always in beta" and that they advertise this fact to users as a promise to be constantly improving. The message also serves as a reminder to employees that change is their norm.

It's a powerful way to think about business. Niccol returned home and talked to his team about having an "always in beta" mind-set. He says it has really "pushed all to be forward-thinking and focused on making history versus talking about history."

∗ Keep the Focus on Your Big Goal

In order to drive through the change you want, you're going to have to keep your Big Goal front and center in your own mind and in the minds of your target audience. The three best ways to keep the focus are through persistence, constant communication, and by playing like you're behind, even when you're not.

PERSISTENCE, PERSISTENCE, PERSISTENCE: In business there can be a lot of diversions and a lot of white noise. It's your job to figure out how to keep the focus on what really matters and not get sidetracked. I've told my board of directors that the moment I stop talking about customer mania, they need to ask for my resignation. We still have a lot of progress to make in terms of satisfying our customers, and if I take my eye off the ball, I know that will signal to the rest of the organization that they can too. And then we'll never get there. As a matter of fact, the focus of my 2011 New Year's message was that we must make operational excellence our number-one business initiative, and I revised all of our major Yum! documents, including our How We Win Together principles, to give it even more emphasis. And even more important, we are revamping our priorities and totally committed to holding people accountable for making significant progress.

I talked before about how great companies have process and discipline around what really matters, around keeping the slots working in Vegas, for example. You've got to have process and discipline too, in terms of applying your own resources—your time, your energy, your know-how—toward getting done what you set out to do.

RELENTLESS COMMUNICATION: Help keep the focus on your goal by never stopping communication with your people. The advertising concept *effective reach* refers to the fact that people don't even begin to be affected by your message until they've heard it at least four times. The same holds true for the leader's message. You have to keep talking about what you want to accomplish, why you want to accomplish it, and how you plan to do it.

I once heard a story about the CEO of Brown & Williamson who was so in love with a new print campaign that the agency had the engraving of the ads framed to hang on his wall. Every day he'd look at these ads while he was in his office until, after some time had passed, he decided it was time to call up his account director. "You know, I think we need a new campaign," he said to him. "This one is wearing out." The account director replied, "What do you mean it's wearing out? Those ads haven't even run yet. We gave you the engravings, but the ads don't hit the magazines until next week."

This is just what leadership is like. We forget how close we are to the thing we're working on, when in truth we are much more focused on it than anyone else around us. That means that even if you think the message you're trying to push through is old news by now, it probably isn't to anyone but you.

When I teach my Taking People with You program, I don't assume that everyone in the room has absorbed it all by the end of our three days together. I follow up to make sure the message is getting through and that people don't return to their offices and just continue with business as usual. I get progress reports on how things are going with their Big Goals after forty days. I send them regular updates in return on how I've been using the lessons of the program to improve my own performance. I do webinars to connect with participants, and I write a regular blog that everyone in the company can read, no matter where they are around the world. As an aside, when I wrote the blog about the birth of my new granddaughter, Audrey Louise Butler, I got more responses by far than on anything else I've ever written. Things like this help make a big company small, and they keep the communication going. You have to figure out ways to keep those channels open between you and your own people.

PLAY AS THOUGH YOU'RE BEHIND: You should be going to work every day believing that you'll succeed, but playing as though you're behind in the score. That's the attitude that will give you the best chance at success. Complacency is one of the biggest killers of any initiative, but if you have it in the back of your mind that your plan

First, everywhere you go in the company, you'll see something on "performance with purpose." Second, every speech I give, I'll relate back to "performance with purpose" in some shape or form. And every one of the senior executives in the company have also learned to talk about "performance with purpose." . . . And then, what we do is every year when we publish the annual report, the consultants always have a new idea for the cover. I told them, "Don't bother. As long as I'm CEO, it's 'performance with purpose.'" So the first year was "Performance with Purpose"; second year was "Performance with Purpose . . . The Journey Continues"; third year was "We Are Performance with Purpose." So it doesn't matter what they suggest, as long as it has the words "performance with purpose."

—INDRA NOOYI, CEO OF PEPSICO

> *It's actually more fun to be an upstart, to be someone people don't expect to be good, and to fight to make it to the major leagues or the Super Bowl. But if you're actually one of the leaders, you have more people kind of attacking you. You can't be arrogant and say, "Well, we're the leader." You have to say to people, "OK, now we're in the major leagues and we want to get to the playoffs, the Super Bowl, every single year." And our discipline has to be, we're going to be faster, tougher, leaner, at a much more disciplined and deeper level, because a lot of people are coming up behind us. When I talk about the competition, I always remind our people they are there and they're coming. And so don't spend a lot of time looking at how well you did in the last game. You should spend a lot of time thinking that they're coming.*
>
> —JAMIE DIMON, CHAIRMAN, PRESIDENT AND CEO, JPMORGAN CHASE

could all fall apart at any moment, then that will keep you sharp. You'll keep looking to identify the unfinished business, keep figuring out what's not working as well as it could and make changes, and keep focused on what's changing in the marketplace that might affect your outcome.

Our China CEO, Sam Su, does this better than any leader I've seen. No matter how much success we've achieved, he and his team constantly challenge one another to raise their game and not settle for the status quo. The result is stellar performance year after year.

The opposite reminds me of the 1948 election, in which Truman won out over Dewey even though the odds against him going in seemed all but hopeless. It wasn't just that Truman outplayed Dewey; it was that, toward the end, Dewey ran his campaign as if it were already in the bag. Both men went on a train tour of the country to connect with voters, but as Truman biographer David McCullough described, "Dewey would travel nowhere near so far, and at a much more leisurely pace. And he would deliver far fewer speeches." In fact, Dewey articulated his point of view to fellow Republican politicians whom he met along the campaign trail—"When you're leading, don't talk," he'd say. Since there is no mention of a President Dewey in any American history textbook, we all know how well that strategy worked out for him. If he had ignored the hype about his inevitable win and campaigned like the one behind in the polls with ground to make up, things just might have been different for him.

tool: self-goading questions

Goad: Something that urges or stimulates action.

Am I stuck in a rut?

Am I destined to produce only *average* results?

Do I subconsciously accept the *status quo* and happily work within it?

Breakthrough performance comes when, even if you are doing well, you develop a healthy dissatisfaction with the status quo. I'm a goader by nature, constantly asking people when something is going to be finished, how they're going to fix problems or improve performance, and so on. But this tool is something I use on myself. I turn that goading instinct inward to make sure I'm not getting complacent. As I've said before, in business there is always unfinished business, more that can be done, more ways to improve. And that's what makes it exciting.

To keep from becoming complacent about the progress you've already made, ask yourself questions like:

What difference am I really making in this area?

How different is my current performance from tens of thousands of people just like me, working on similar projects in thousands of other organizations?

Am I really doing anything special, or am I kidding myself?

Am I really aiming to make a big difference, or am I fooling myself and aiming for just a bit better?

Will there really be anything about my efforts that I will be proud to share with my spouse or my children?

© John O'Keeffe, BusinessBeyondtheBox.com

You know, one of the hardest things to do is to stay motivated yourself. And the way I've found to stay motivated is to make sure I have people around me always who are better, smarter, quicker, more capable. They'll keep you on your toes. And you keep asking yourself, "Well, why are they better, smarter, faster?" Because if you can't find any answers to those, I think it's time to move out of the way. When you can find the answers, then you'll find what your needs are and you'll start addressing your needs.

—BOB HOLLAND, MANAGING DIRECTOR AND ADVISORY BOARD MEMBER, ESSEX LAKE GROUP

✳ Change Lovers Wanted

Jim Collins told me that, while he was doing research for his book *Good to Great,* he talked to an executive about how his company had become a great company, and the executive said, "To understand, you really have to understand one thing: You can delight us but you can never satisfy us." What that means, Collins explained to me, is that "every time the bar gets to this level, then we're done with that bar, and the bar just goes up again. It's a never-ending process. And you go back to the question of the right people versus the wrong people. The right people are the ones who really like that."

Our CEO of Pizza Hut, Scott Bergren, calls this being a change junkie, and it's the best sort of person to surround yourself with. It's also the kind of person you want to be yourself. Golf coach Bob Rotella once told me what he admired most about the great Jack Nicklaus. He said, "What I was so impressed with about Nicklaus was that he sustained his hunger for a good thirty years. He was not only unbelievably hungry when he was poor and hadn't won anything, he was unbelievably motivated and hungry when he was extremely wealthy and successful and everyone was kissing his butt. The amazing thing was that he sustained it."

You'll know that you've surrounded yourself with the right people and that you're doing a good job of getting through to them when your own messages start coming back to you. I mentioned before how happy Tom Ryan of CVS/Caremark was when his employees told him that they sat in the same place for lunch every day because it was "easy and effective." That's how he knew his efforts to communicate the company's new vision were working. A similar thing happened to me not long ago at a year-end investor meeting. Just a few weeks before, *Fortune* magazine had rated me number fourteen on their list of the top people in business. I viewed it as a team honor, because the only reason I was on the list was because of the hard work of our people, which is what has driven our successful track record. But what meant more to me personally was when Rick Carucci, our CFO, stopped his investor presentation to give me his personal recognition award. He calls it his Show Me the Money Award, and it consists of a transparent piggy bank and a copy of the movie *Jerry McGuire* (where the phrase *show me the money* comes from).

While it was awkward and a bit embarrassing to be recognized in front of investors, I was proud to be on the receiving end of the kind of recognition I had started seventeen years ago when I gave out my first floppy chicken. I was even more pleased to see that Rick felt

> *If you run a marathon, you've got to put in weeks and weeks of training. The difference between a good runner and a great runner is, the great runner goes out on days when the good runner chooses to sleep in or stay home. When you look at someone's career, and it's certainly true with mine, nothing happens in a linear way. There are years where you go sideways. There are times when you go backward and get frustrated. But the ability to come in every day and try to do the best you can and try to keep moving forward, that's what creates opportunities. Success comes in a lumpy way.*
>
> —STEVE BURKE, CEO OF NBCUNIVERSAL AND AVID RUNNER

comfortable enough to have a little fun with me during an otherwise pretty formal investor meeting. After he gave me his award, he did a Letterman-style slide presentation of the top five reasons why I'd made the list, including because "only fifteen people had filled out the form" and because I'd had "lots of help from the CFO." The number-one reason he gave was that I'd "scored high in the swimsuit and talent competitions" accompanied by a not-so-flattering picture. Investor meetings are typically pretty serious affairs, and it was nice to see everyone having a good laugh, even if it was at my expense. I've learned that there's a universal desire to be recognized, and I guess I'm no exception. It still means a lot to be thanked for what I do. It was a great example of taking people with me and of our culture working the way I'd always envisioned it would. After all the hard work I'd put into it, it was as if Rick were telling me publicly: Message received.

tool: "tomorrow is the first day of . . ."

	TODAY ⇒ Status Quo	TOMORROW ⇒ First day of . . .	REST OF MY . . . . . . Career
. . My time with my partner			
. . . My time with my children			

What will you do differently to make it to breakthrough? It's never too late to raise your performance or make changes in anything you do.

Use this tool to free your mind and push toward the future by asking yourself:

If tomorrow was a completely new start to this project, what would I do differently? What breathtaking results can I imagine? How can I start making those happen today?

© John O'Keeffe, BusinessBeyondtheBox.com

* Insights and Actions

Self-reflection

Assess yourself on the following items related to chapter 14, "The Change Is Never Over":	Personal Opportunity	Personal Strength
1. I am persistent in achieving commitments.		
2. I am able to spot problems early and galvanize my team to address them.		
3. I regularly check my dissatisfaction with the status quo to identify new challenges.		
4. I recognize the need to adjust a course of action based on new knowledge or circumstances.		
5. I remain positive even when times are tough.		
6. I continually work to keep my life balanced, taking time to rest and recharge.		

Exercise

Think of the day-to-day effort you put into your Big Goal. How many days of the week are you absolutely *full on* toward your challenge? How many days are spent being just so-so toward your Big Goal?

What can you do to eliminate the time you spend in the So-So Zone?

* Learning Download for Part III: Follow Through to Get Results

• It's not just what you say, it's how you say it. You have to sell people on your goal, **market the change,** the same way you would if you were selling a new product to a customer. The more compelling you make it for people, the more willing they will be to help you accomplish your Big Goal.

• With any goal, there are **barriers to success you'll need to overcome.** You have to make sure you've heard from everyone about what they think the issues are, because they might see things that you don't.

• You need to measure the progress you make toward achieving your goal to make sure you're on the right track. **Recognizing** the progress you're making along the way and those who are doing an outstanding job will motivate people to see it through.

• Real success comes from recognizing that there is always more to know and more to do and that the leader can never let up. The **change is never over,** and that applies equally to growing your business and growing yourself.

To further reflect on these lessons and put them to work for you, go back through your answers to the Exercises and Self-Reflection questions at the end of each chapter. Next, answer the following questions, which will help you determine where you need to focus your efforts the most as you build your skills as a leader.

• What are the biggest aha's you picked up about yourself while reading the chapters in part 3, "Follow Through to Get Results"?

• Of those aha's, what are the two or three that, if you worked on them, would have the greatest impact on your Big Goal?

- What will you start doing differently tomorrow as a result of what you've learned in this section?

Once again, the stories that follow are from people who have been through my leadership program and have had their own difficulties in maximizing their potential in a particular area. I hope you'll take some inspiration from how Cheryl and Keith did something about those things that were difficult for them.

Cheryl on "Market the Change"

I was really disappointed when, over the course of several years' worth of performance reviews, I kept receiving the same feedback, which was that I didn't come across as having enough positive energy. It really hit home for me when I was interviewing a potential new hire. In interviews, I'm always effusive about our culture, and this time was no different. I was going on and on about what a positive place this is to work, about how everyone believed in making work fun, and how that drove high levels of achievement. As I was talking, it suddenly hit home that I was a "bad ad" for the kind of culture I was supposed to be promoting as an HR leader. So a few days later, I did something a little extreme to jolt myself out of this state and to get others to start seeing me differently. At the start of a department meeting, in order to get everyone's attention, I spontaneously started doing this callback cheer. I yelled out to my group, "I'm fired up, how about you?" And they responded, "We're fired up, how about you?" It was pretty goofy, but everyone laughed, and the energy level in the room went up immediately. Plus, I instantly had everyone's focused attention, so we could start the meeting. Now I do this cheer every time I (or someone in my department) need a boost. It helps keep me positive, and I can already tell that people are responding differently to me.

Keith on "Some People Will Say It Can't Be Done"

I'm a natural consensus builder. I love to facilitate open and frank discussions with my team. But the flip side of that is that I'm pretty nonconfrontational. I've never been very comfortable with negativity or conflict, so I have a tendency to just ignore it. This came up recently because my team and I were working on a big project and we were making good progress, except for one guy who kept saying that the whole thing was a waste of time. He'd thought that from the beginning, and he'd told us all why, but we decided to go ahead anyway. He just wouldn't let it drop. Every meeting we had about the project, he'd say something about how he could be doing better things with his time. Finally, I didn't feel as though I had a choice; I went to HR and got him reassigned.

The big lesson for me was how much credibility I gained in the eyes of my team as a result. I'd been worried that they would think I'd been too harsh or, worse, that they would worry about the stability of their own positions as a result. But it was exactly the opposite. They really appreciated what I'd done. One of them even said that it felt as though I'd stuck up for them by getting rid of this guy, which, I realized, is exactly how I want them to feel.

afterword

be your own big goal: move from me to we

m y challenge to you, as you finish reading this book, is to avoid falling back into business as usual. Instead, I hope you'll take this opportunity to do things differently and that you'll view this, not as the end of a book, but as a launching pad for a new way of thinking and a new way of leading.

Go back, for a moment, to the tool I introduced to you in chapter 1, Picture Step-Change. That tool asks you to think about progress not as a series of small steps, but as potentially big leaps forward. Think about how you might be able to apply that kind of thinking to what you've learned in this book. Typically you probably read a business book, take a few nuggets of wisdom from it, and then put it back on the shelf, only to largely forget about it. But what if this time around, things were different? What if you really could make big strides—or step-changes—in your life and career, starting from where you are right now?

If you want that to happen, you're going to have to set some Big Goals for yourself in terms of what you want to get out of this book. The way I see it, you now have *two* big projects to work on: The first is the Big Goal you set for yourself in chapter 1, and the second project is you. You can either take small steps or you can make big leaps forward in both these areas. The choice is entirely up to you.

When working on the project that is you, I encourage you to think about it the same way you would about achieving any goal: Identify what you want to change, make a plan for improving yourself and your skills, set deadlines and benchmarks, and seek out feedback and help.

I think it actually makes perfect sense to work on these two projects in tandem, because doing bigger things and being a better you go hand in hand. You really can't do one without the other.

* From Me to We

There is a story from my career that I think is a perfect metaphor for how being a better you makes you better at what you do. When I was at PepsiCo, we used to work with a lot of celebrities. One of the most memorable was the basketball player Magic Johnson. We were one of his sponsors when he announced to the world that he was HIV positive. The news came as quite a shock, and a number of his sponsors dropped him soon afterward. We got a call from his agent saying that he and Magic wanted to come to New York to talk with Craig Weatherup, the head of PepsiCo at the time, and me. They wanted to know if we were going to hang in there with Magic.

The ease with which Craig and I made the decision was striking to me. We both knew what we believed was the right thing to do, and we did it without looking back. So right up front, we told Magic that we wanted to keep working with him. With that out of the way, we got the rare opportunity to just sit and talk with the guy.

One of the first things I wanted to know was what it was like for him growing up. I mean, he was one of the best athletes in the entire NBA. I could only imagine what it was like when he was playing in high school.

"Well," he said, "when I first started playing as a kid, we'd win by these huge margins, like 80 to 20. And I'd score like 65 of those points. The problem was, even though we were winning, no one was happy. The other kids weren't happy, their parents weren't happy, and as a result, I wasn't happy either.

"All of a sudden, I realized that the best way to fix things was to get more people involved. So I made the decision to become the best passer that I could possibly be. After that, we didn't win by as big a margin, but we still won. The score would be more like 70 to 30, and I'd score only about 40 of those points while the rest of the team scored about 30. But everyone was participating, everyone was making shots, and everyone was happy."

When Magic went to the NBA, his goal was to have more passing assists than any other player in history. He told his teammate on the Lakers Kareem Abdul Jabbar that he was going to help him become the leading scorer in the league, which he did. He told his teammate James Worthy that he was going to help him make the All-Star team for the first time; that happened too. Teammate Byron Scott ended up with more three-pointers than any other player, and Magic set him up for a bunch of them. When Kareem scored the point that broke the record, making him the leading scorer of all time in the NBA, he went straight over to Magic to hug him. And then he said to him, "You told me you'd do it. You told me."

"That," Magic said, "was the greatest thing."

Afterward, I thought a lot about that story and what it meant from a leadership perspective. Magic, I realized, had learned early the power of taking people with him. He chose the team over himself, and he made things better for everyone, including himself, as a result.

That, essentially, is what leadership is all about. There are really two ways to think of your growth as a leader: You can practice your hook shot over and over again until you can practically make it in your sleep, or you can work on being great at the assist, at setting up others to make their shots alongside you.

That doesn't mean Magic couldn't make a shot when he needed to. I vividly remember watching a game in which Kareem was hurt, so Magic took over his position as center. Now Magic was used to playing guard, but he rose to the occasion, making all kinds of shots to lead his team to victory against the Boston Celtics. But Magic was truly at his best when he was supporting his team members and taking them along with him.

I truly believe that taking people with you is *the* job of every leader; it's not something that can be delegated. I hope I've shown in the preceding pages how crucial it is to the success of your business that you think of the people you work with in the same way that Magic Johnson thought about his teammates. If you're one person getting big things done, that's pretty good, but it will take you only so far. If you can help a whole team or organization full of people to reach big goals, then there's no telling what you can accomplish together. It's up to you as a leader to make that happen.

As I close this book, I'm reminded of something I witnessed not long ago while traveling. It was Saturday morning, and I was reading the paper outside by the pool at my hotel. I looked up and saw a woman walk over to the pool. She stuck her toe in the cool water and then very gradually started to lower herself in, inch by inch. It was actually pretty funny to watch, because it was taking her so long to make any progress. She shivered and grimaced the whole time even though she was barely making a dent in the pool.

Meanwhile, a young kid ran past her and jumped right in, cannonball-style. He made a huge splash that got everyone's attention and resulted in ripples that went from one side of the pool to the other. It seems to me that you have a choice. You can take the lessons you've learned from this book and dabble with them from time to time, which will probably not make that much difference in your life or in others'. Or you can jump in with abandon, put these lessons to work, and create ripples that will help you and those around you achieve all that you're capable of. I hope you'll choose to be a ripple maker and receive all the joy and results that go with it.

acknowledgments

The origin of this book stems from the Taking People with You leadership program I've had the privilege of teaching to over four thousand Yum! leaders and franchisees. So first, I'd like to thank all of you who have attended the program and followed the road map. Collectively, you have applied the lessons of this program and achieved the kind of results that give this book credibility. I especially want to thank the many of you who asked me at the end of the program, "Why don't you write a book?," which inspired me to actually do it.

Speaking of the program, I want to thank Tim Galbraith, who has been my program development partner the past fourteen years. He has helped me constantly improve the seminar and this book with his creative ideas and substantive input. I would also like to thank my current chief people officer, Anne Byerlein, and past human resources leaders, Gregg Dedrick and Peter Hearl, for helping me teach the class. They traveled the globe with me, bringing positive energy and insight to every session.

Now on to the book. It's been an absolute joy working with Christa Bourg, who has helped me write this book. She attended my program several times, understood exactly what we wanted to communicate, and captured my voice. She added tremendous value and worked tirelessly to get the best possible product. If you liked the book, she deserves much of the credit. I also want to thank my literary agent, Jim Levine, and publisher, Adrian Zackheim, both whom constantly demonstrated why they are acknowledged to be the best in their respective businesses. Jonathan Blum, my partner, friend, and chief public affairs officer, was instrumental in bringing this A-Team to the party and helped me make the book what it is.

I've had the incredible blessing of being exposed to the best and brightest, so I once again want to acknowledge the "cast of experts" and the Yum! Brands board of directors. I truly appreciate how you so willingly shared your know-how with me and now with the readers of this book. I especially want to thank John O'Keeffe for allowing me to share his Business Beyond the Box tools. John's tools, along with those provided by Larry Senn, help make this book interactive and inspire personal reflection.

I've also been fortunate to have worked for a number of world-class coaches: Jim Walczy, Tom James, Howard Davis, Steve Reinemund, Craig Weatherup, Roger Enrico, the late Wayne Calloway, and the late Andrall Pearson. In particular, it was the highlight of my career to be mentored by Andy, who not only passed on his considerable knowledge, but was my very best pal when he passed away at eighty years young.

I want to thank my family. Jean and Charles Novak are the kind of loving and encouraging parents you could only dream of. My wife, Wendy, is an incredible partner and challenged me to make this book better. Last but not least, I want to thank my daughter, Ashley Novak Butler, who read each chapter from the vantage point of an up-and-coming leader, and gave me invaluable input on how to make the book more meaningful and relevant for leaders at every level.

God has blessed me with a life filled with amazing experiences and incredible people. It's been a true joy to pass on what I've learned over the years to you. Thank you for buying this book, all the profits from which are going to the United Nations World Food Programme in our ongoing effort to save the lives of starving kids around the world.

Moataz al-Alfi—CEO, Egypt Kuwait Holding, and chairman of the board, Americana Group, Egypt

Graham Allan—CEO, Yum! Restaurants International

Scott Bergren—CEO of Pizza Hut, United States

Ken Blanchard—cofounder and chief spiritual officer, the Ken Blanchard Companies; author

Lawrence Bossidy—former vice chairman, General Electric; former CEO, AlliedSignal

Jamie Brunner—founder, Kinetix Nutrition and Fitness

Warren Buffett—chairman and CEO, Berkshire Hathaway

Stephen Burke—CEO, NBCUniversal

John Calipari—men's basketball coach, University of Kentucky

Jim Collins—business author (*Built to Last* and *Good to Great*)

David Cote—CEO, Honeywell International

Greg Creed—CEO, Taco Bell, United States

Jamie Dimon—chairman, president, and CEO, JPMorgan Chase & Co.

David Dorman—chairman of the board and presiding director, Motorola, Inc.

Howard C. Draft—executive chairman, Draftfcb

Roger Eaton—CEO, KFC, United States

Massimo Ferragamo—chairman, Ferragamo USA, Inc.

Michael Francis—executive vice president and chief marketing officer, Target Corp.

David Grissom—chairman, Mayfair Capital, and chairman, Glenview Trust

Bonnie Hill—president, B. Hill Enterprises

Bob Holland—managing director and advisory board member, Essex Lake Group

Jeffrey Immelt—chairman and CEO, General Electric

Kenneth Langone—president and CEO, Invemed Associates; cofounder, Home Depot

Jon Linen—adviser to the chairman, American Express Company

Alan Mulally—CEO, Ford Motor Co.

Thomas C. Nelson—president and CEO, National Gypsum Company

Indra Nooyi—chairman and CEO, PepsiCo

John O'Keeffe—creator and author of *Business Beyond the Box*

Micky Pant—president of global branding, Yum! Brands

Andrall Pearson—late founding chairman and CEO, Yum! Brands

Lee Raymond—former chairman and CEO, ExxonMobil

Bob Rotella—sports psychologist and author of *Golf Is Not a Game of Perfect*

Thomas Ryan—former chairman, president, and CEO, Caremark Pharmacy Services, CVS Caremark Corporation

Howard Schultz—chairman, president, and CEO, Starbucks

Larry Senn—chairman and founder of Senn Delaney; expert on corporate culture

Jim Stengel—president and CEO of the Jim Stengel Company; adjunct professor, Anderson School of Management, UCLA

Randall Stephenson—chairman and CEO, AT&T

Sam Su—vice chairman of Yum! Brands, chairman and CEO of Yum! China

Noel Tichy—professor of organizational behavior and human resource management, Ross School of Business, University of Michigan

Bob Walter—former chairman and CEO, Cardinal Health, Inc.

Jack Welch—founder, Jack Welch Management Institute; former chairman and CEO, General Electric

William Weldon—chairman and CEO, Johnson & Johnson

John Wooden—late Hall of Fame basketball coach, UCLA

index